CW00644467

TRANSIENT

TRANSIENT

THE BRIDGE BETWEEN WORLDS

INDAH GUNAWAN

NEW DEGREE PRESS

COPYRIGHT © 2021 INDAH GUNAWAN

All rights reserved.

TRANSIENT

The Bridge Between Worlds

ISBN   978-1-63676-928-8   *Paperback*

            978-1-63676-992-9   *Kindle Ebook*

            978-1-63730-096-1   *Ebook*

I've always said this as a bit of a joke: "You know, if all else fails in my life, I can just write a book about all the crazy shit I've lived through as an international student." Seeing as how you're currently reading these words, I guess it's not a joke anymore.

CONTENTS

INTRODUCTION. TRANSIENT IN NATURE   **9**

PART I.   **FIRST DAY BASICS**   **17**

CHAPTER 1. "HELLO, MY NAME IS ___"   21

CHAPTER 2. "OH, YOUR ENGLISH IS SO GOOD!"   39

CHAPTER 3. THE FAULT IN THE COOKIE CUTTER   59

PART II.   **ANGLOSPECTIVE**   **77**

CHAPTER 4. THE INTERNATIONAL CHALLENGE TO WESTERN DOMINANCE   81

CHAPTER 5. ALL AROUND THE WORLD IN A FEW DISHES   101

CHAPTER 6. THE CULTURAL PARADIGMS OF EDUCATION   119

CHAPTER 7. BIRDS OF A FEATHER FLOCK TOGETHER   143

PART III.   **THE POLITICS OF LIVING IN BETWEEN**   **159**

CHAPTER 8. RELATIONSHIPS IN TRANSIT   163

CHAPTER 9. THE BEST OF BOTH WORLDS   179

CHAPTER 10. THE REAL CULTURE SHOCK   195

PART IV.   **FINAL STRETCH**   **207**

CHAPTER 11. "SORRY, WE DON'T SPONSOR INTERNATIONAL STUDENTS"   211

CHAPTER 12. THE BRIDGE BETWEEN WORLDS   231

SPECIAL ACKNOWLEDGMENTS   **241**

APPENDIX   **247**

INTRODUCTION

TRANSIENT IN NATURE

"International student" generally can be one or both of two things: someone who attended an international school at any point during their K–12 years (whether it's in their domestic country, or in other foreign countries), or someone who traveled outside of their home country to pursue their tertiary education abroad (e.g., colleges, universities, technical training institutes). In my case, I was both, and that's exactly what this book has been inspired by—my personal life growing up in Jakarta, Indonesia as a third-culture kid going to international schools, and my four years of college as an international student in Los Angeles, California.

A term coined by US sociologist Ruth Hill Useem in the 1950s, a "third-culture kid" (TCK) is someone who develops an identity rooted more in people rather than places. They are citizens of everywhere, and nowhere, at the same time. Traditionally, TCKs were those who spent their formative years in countries outside of their parents' homeland—most of them being children of expatriate workers—but in a world where industrialization and globalization have increasingly blurred the lines between cultures all around the world, that identity has expanded to encompass children who come from transnational marriages, as well as children who attended international schools in their home countries.[1]

I think for a lot of people these days, when they hear the term "international student," they typically picture some spoiled rich kid who graduated from a prestigious, super expensive private high school back in their home country. They have millionaire or billionaire parents who pay for their entire college tuition and living expenses abroad (and normally in either the United States, Canada, Australia, or the United Kingdom), so they essentially get to just have fun and blow their parents' money all day. They live their lives like they're on the cast of *Crazy Rich Asians* or *Bling Empire*. They drive to campus in cars that cost more than what some of their professors make in a year and the clothes and accessories they wear to class are probably worth more than your entire closet. *Even their dogs get to sit with them in first class on the flight back home.* After graduation, they'll most likely end up going back to either take over the family business or start their own venture funded by mommy and daddy.

Oh, and they probably don't speak English.

In reality, international students have such a diverse plethora of stories and experiences. Not all of us went to private schools, or even international schools, back home. Some of us don't come from wealthy families, and some can barely afford tuition. Not all of us experience being homesick because some of us don't even know where "home" is. Some of us don't feel at home where home should be because some

---

1   Kate Mayberry, "Third Culture Kids: Citizens of everywhere and nowhere," *BBC,* November 19, 2016.

of us don't fully identify with the culture of our parents, or where we grew up. Some of us grew up in one country, while others have never stayed in one country for more than a few years. Some will eventually come back home to their parents, while others intend on permanently moving elsewhere in search of a new life. Some of us will be allowed to stay in our host countries after graduation, while others will be forced to pack up their things and leave. The list goes on. We all come from different walks of life, but the one thing that has led us down to the same path—regardless of culture, language, religion, gender, or even wealth—is we have to figure out how to be both the new student in class and the new foreigner in town all at the same time. One way or another, we have all been forced to grow up much faster than other kids in our age groups. We've had to learn how to say goodbye to friends and family, travel across vast oceans, and live in a foreign country all alone—all at such a young age, with little to no time to sit down and process everything into something that makes sense.

Oh, and by the way, most of us do speak English.

These are tales and adventures we don't often find represented, and when there is a lack of proper representation of a certain group, that gap creates misconceptions that compartmentalize an entire demographic into one homogenous monolith. I want to show there is so much more to being an international student than just what the stereotypes say about us. So many of our stories are cool, funny, wild, and amazing, but so many of them are also unfair, disappointing, complicated, and traumatic. Nobody can deny the amount of privilege that comes with being an international student, but that doesn't take away from the confusions and hardships that come with it as well.

This book is filled with a wide array of stories about navigating the third-culture kid identity: figuring out cross-cultural relationships at school and at home, dealing with culture shock, discrimination, prejudice, employment and immigration struggles, and much more. I want to give an honest reckoning of my time as an Indonesian international student in America, and the events and people who shaped those four years. I want to share with you my insights into some of the ups and downs most international students often go through by not only sharing my own personal journey, but by also sharing the tales of other international students I've had the chance to survey and interview from all over the world. These are students who, like me, came from foreign cultures in pursuit of collegiate- and master's-level education in the United States, Canada, Australia, and the United Kingdom (simply referred to as **"the anglosphere"** from here on out). You will also get to hear from former international students, like actor and comedian Ronny Chieng, as well as US Senator of Illinois Tammy Duckworth.

Most chapters are immediately followed by "accompanying chapters" which feature stories and insights from other international students whose surveys and interview responses I've quoted to feature in this book. Consider these accompanying inserts supplementary, and completely optional for you to read. That being said, I implore you, as the reader, to please not dismiss these stories and the time people have taken to share them. As much as this book is dedicated to giving volume to stories and experiences that often go unheard, it's also dedicated to honoring the emotions behind them as well.

The only chapters without these accompanying chapters are the final chapter, as well as chapters eight, nine, and ten under the chapter subheading "The Politics of Living in Between." I imagine you'd have questions as to why. I would be lying if I said getting survey responses and interview sign-ups for those three chapters in particular haven't been the most difficult. In part, I realized, it was perhaps due to the incredibly sensitive and subjective nature of the topics discussed. Additionally, if I'd had more time to work on this book and perhaps find more people who were willing to discuss such intimate subjects, I would have loved to feature them in here, but alas, *it do be like that sometimes.* Nevertheless, in spite of the lack of quotes from other students, and it mainly serving as an excuse for me to vent about the *unfairness and injustices of my life,* I hope you find these three chapters insightful, if not at least entertaining to read.

* * *

Although international students who studied in the US, UK, Canada, and Australia (who are not originally from these group of countries mentioned) make up the majority of the survey and interview participants, other participants include: expatriates from the anglosphere who have spent at least six months living as either students or workers in a foreign country, first-generation immigrants who immigrated to the anglosphere from another culture, domestic students from the anglosphere who have taken part in at least six months of study abroad or foreign exchange programs, and domestic students from the anglosphere pursuing a collegiate- or master's-level education in another foreign country. Note that survey and interview responses from some of these listed participants are also included in this book in the form of quotations. Many of our journeys inherently intersect those who are immigrants, minorities, mixed-race, and other types of foreigner backgrounds, and I really do think this inclusivity is perhaps one of the most beautiful things about this book.

So much of our experiences as international students are transient in nature. Culture shock, homesickness, and loneliness don't last forever, but neither do our friendships, relationships, or the places we call home. We say goodbye to one person, and we immediately say hello to another. One day we wake up in one city, and that same night we go to bed in another. We're always something in between, never anything in particular; we're always everywhere, yet nowhere at the same time. Sometimes it leaves you feeling empty, but other times it leaves you feeling full.

DISCLAIMERS

First disclaimer: This book talks about what it's like to be an international student in the anglosphere. That being said, *I've* only ever lived in the United States. For the most part, I can only speak on *my* experience as an international student *there*. The parts where I do speak on behalf of other countries in the anglosphere, I made sure to support any general statements or findings with proper evidence and citation. None of the experiences and opinions shared by me, or any other participant quoted in this book, are meant to reflect every single international student out there.

Second disclaimer: "Anglosphere" countries encompass the United States, the United Kingdom, Canada, Australia, New Zealand, the Republic of Ireland, and Commonwealth Caribbean countries like the Bahamas, Barbados, and Jamaica. Note the nations included can vary according from source to source. The US, Canada, Australia, New Zealand, and the UK make up what's known as the "Core Anglosphere," but as previously mentioned, I simply refer to them as "the anglosphere" from here on out. Also, New Zealand is unfortunately not included in this book. Can you believe out of the three hundred sixty-three students who signed up as survey and/or interview participants for this book from all over the world, *none of them happened to have studied in New Zealand?* Granted, they are a very small country with an even smaller population of international students because most people who decide to study abroad in the West typically choose to go to the US, Canada, UK, or Australia—and understandably so.

These four countries not only host some of the best and most prestigious higher academic institutions globally, but they are also on the top ten list of countries hosting the greatest number of international students from all over the world. The reason why I wanted to talk about these four countries, instead of just the US, is because all four of them share a common historical narrative and maintain close cultural affinities with one another. I not only wanted to see the contrast in the journeys of international students from this group of countries, but I also wanted to compare the similar stories and experiences and see what bigger meaning could be derived from all those.

Third disclaimer: I am just one person. I can't possibly talk about *every single thing* there has to do with being an international student because that experience within itself varies per individual. Every story is different; mine is only one out of many. Understand this book is largely just a recount of *my* life, where I'm sharing the journey of being an international student through *my* lens in hopes some things would resonate with some people. Not everything I talk about in this book is going to be relatable to everyone, and that's okay.

Fourth disclaimer: If you picked up this book expecting to find sophisticated literary work the likes of Virginia Woolf, you're in for a whole lot of disappointment. Take everything I say in this book with a grain of salt—don't take it too personally or seriously—because honestly, I'm just a nobody. I'm not even one-year post-undergrad. I wrote this book within the pink Hello-Kitty enshrouded comforts of my childhood bedroom after being forced to come back to Jakarta in the middle of my final semester of college because of a raging global pandemic that's basically screwed the entire world, *and nobody wanted to hire me.*

Fifth disclaimer: I like to think I am a very funny and animated individual, and I try to show as much of that side of me in this book as possible. I want you to read this and feel like you're sitting down with a friend, having a heart-to-heart conversation that goes from really deep and serious one moment, to stupid and hilarious in another. That being said, I have a very—for a lack of a better word—*crass* sense of humor, and I understand it will not tickle everybody's funny bone. Some of you are going to read this and think *"sheesh, tone down the attitude,"* which is perfectly valid, but that's just who I am as a person. If you have a problem with that *then you can go and fuck yourse*—I'm kidding. In case you couldn't tell from the fact I've already dropped two curse words and we're only at the introduction of this book, I have the mouth of an emotionally constipated sailor *and mother **will** clutch her pearls.* If swearing, and the humor of a pre-pubescent eleven year old, turn you off in any way, I apologize, but you're here now, and I've already taken your money, so you might as well just sit back and enjoy the ride I'm about to take you on.

FIRST DAY BASICS

English names are becoming increasingly common in order for people to "fit in" with the Western world, in hopes we will be accepted for who we are and not have that be swayed by what we're called.

—JASON TAITE | HONG KONG, CHINA, & SINGAPORE

CHAPTER 1

"HELLO, MY NAME IS ___"

IN-DUH GOO-NUH-WON

I've had to learn from an early age that some people have a different experience of how they walk through the world depending on the names they are given. They say not to judge a book by its cover, but the truth is people already have formed some level of an opinion about you just by looking at your name. You probably did so too while reading my name on the cover of this book. You've probably tried to gauge the appeal of this book solely based on the title of it as well. Many of our first impressions are based on what something, or someone, is called. Whether it's for products, objects, or people, names are the foundation of how we are treated by the world.

I spent every day of the first fifteen years of my life being called the wrong name by everyone. No, really, *everyone*— my friends, my teachers, and even my own mom. I'm twenty-four years old today and everybody knows me as *Indah Gunawan*, but that identity never formally existed until only nine years ago. Gunawan is my mom's legal surname, and an adopted surname for me at best, because Indonesian family names are legally patronymic, which becomes an issue if you grew up without a dad like I did. When I was in kindergarten, a teacher made the mistake of introducing me as *Putri*, which legally was supposed to be a middle name but ended up becoming a surname instead, and ever since then, that's what everybody knew me as, including my mom. What a shit-show, I know. I was just a kid and didn't know I could— *should*—have corrected people for calling me by the wrong name. I didn't, though, and I ended up paying the price for my lack of actions years later when I was dealing with the problem of being known as somebody I didn't want to be known as.

By fourth grade, I started to notice how I was one of the few kids in class who did not have a "normal name," which I always understood to mean an *English name*—ones you can find on a personalized name keychain at souvenir stores or share with a celebrity or a character from TV. I dreaded the start of every school year whenever there was a new teacher or student. Somebody was always going to butcher my name because some names, like mine, just never sounded right when said in an anglicized pronunciation. The kids at school caught onto how the name *Putri* sounds like saying *poo tree* in English, which inspired a series of poop-themed nicknames and insults that haunted me throughout my entire adolescence. A teacher's computer's auto-correct mistake, ironically, changed my last name to *Putrid*, and suddenly everybody made jokes about how I smelled bad. To some of you reading this, all of this might seem somewhat comedic. Some of my classmates may even still look back at these memories and laugh about the good old days when we were in elementary school and middle school, but now I'm a college graduate. I'm a grown adult, and I'm still trying to reconcile with the same traumas I've harbored about my name since childhood.

My mother couldn't understand why I hated my name so much and always scolded me for it. Names are more than just a representation of where we come from. They carry the stories of our cultures, our families, and represent messages of qualities, strengths, hopes, and dreams our parents wish for us to embody as we grow older—and we *should* be proud of it. To those who understand the Indonesian language, the message for me is pretty obvious. *Indah* means *beautiful* and *Putri* means *princess.* Cheesy, I know, but I'm not going to lie, it's also quite endearing. Not like it mattered anyway, because I went to an international school where that message unfortunately fell onto deaf ears.

I was entering ninth grade when I transferred to a different international school, and that's when I started going by the moniker *Indah Gunawan.* Arguably, it's far more palatable for English speakers to pronounce. I had already learned from experience adapting the pronunciation of my name in an English-speaking environment was necessary for survival. Even if I didn't have an English name, I could at least make that name pass by just pronouncing it in a more English way. Nobody in high school had anything bad to say about the name *In-Duh Goo-Nuh-Won,* and I never ran into misspelling or mispronunciation issues either, which was fortunate. That being said, I had the luxury of being in a multicultural environment where people were better accustomed to foreign names. That did not seem to be the case when I finally moved to the United States for college.

SO, HOW DO YOU PRONOUNCE YOUR NAME?

Whenever someone reads my name for the first time, they always struggle with how to pronounce it. At the start of every class, I always notice the sudden shift in tone, *even facial expressions*, whenever professors get to a foreign name on the roster. An immediate visible sense of intimidation and discomfort from a name they have never seen or heard of before becomes noticeable, and often times this is how I know I'm the one who is about to be called on next. They would try to sound it out before either stopping to ask, *"How do you pronounce your name?"* or give up midway, which was always my cue to swoop in and say it for them. *"In-duh,"* I say to them, making sure to enunciate it clearly.

It is not wrong to first ask people how their names are pronounced or spelled. On the contrary, it is preferable that you do. Not only is it courteous, but it also saves the other person the embarrassment of being called the wrong name. I speak from personal experience of having everybody constantly mistake my name for *India*. On better days, they think it's *Linda* or *Indie*. Sometimes I think it's almost as if their brains come with an auto-correct feature that sees my name as a spelling mistake, and so they change it to the closest English word they can think of. One time I received an email from an AT&T customer service representative, and instead of addressing it to *Indah Gunawan Putri,* it somehow auto corrected my name to *India Guinea Pig.*

Admittedly, this incident has turned out to be one of my funniest stories that gets the most laughs from people, so I can't even be mad about it. The worst incident where I did get mad, however, was at my business honor society induction ceremony. While all of the inductees were lined up, getting ready to receive our certificates and induction pins, everybody's names got called, except for mine. *So I just stood there, like a clueless idiot, in front of hundreds of people looking at me like I was a puppy at an animal shelter waiting to get adopted.* Later that night, I received an apology email explaining to me what had happened. The computer system erased my name because someone had misspelled it, and it didn't match the name on the official inductees list.

* * *

Whenever people ask me how I pronounce my name, there's always a few seconds of me wondering which version of it I should give them, or which version they are looking for. Being raised in an English-speaking environment has made me accustomed to *only* saying my name the *"white way,"* so when some people ask me for the Indonesian way of saying it, even I sometimes forget how to pronounce it. Other times, I'm just conflicted whether I should tell them the proper pronunciation just so they are aware, or let it go because I don't want to be seen as someone who makes a big deal out of something seemingly miniscule. We live in a society that prioritizes convenience over correctness. It may not be entirely accurate, but as long as it gets the job done, it's okay. We do this with a lot of things, and pronunciation of names are no exception. Personally, I equally settle for both versions. It always just feels like I have two different names, and I have to be conscious of where I am and with whom I am speaking to know which pronunciation to use.

Now I kind of feel weird whenever I introduce myself with the non-English pronunciation of my name. I know it's a shame that I do, but I just feel weird standing out that way.

—MIRA KURTOVIC | HUNGARY & BOSNIA-HERZEGOVINA

I have a bad habit of just going along with others' pronunciations because it's easier. Most people ask if it's the correct pronunciation, however some of those people then proceed to forget. I've corrected one of my university lecturers on how to say my name, but he would just constantly forget. I didn't want to keep correcting him because I felt bad telling him he's always wrong, so I just went with it for the full five months of the semester. If he's teaching me next year, I'm just going to go with it. If he realizes he's been saying it wrong the whole time, then that's another talk for another time.

—MAIKA KUMADA | JAPAN

My name was always a conversation starter for every new person I met, even during the moments where I wish it wasn't. For the most part, I don't mind it. It's just that I'm not always in a situation or mood where I want, or even have the time, to explain *what it means* and *where it's originally from.* This then leads them to ask more complicated questions like *"Where are you from?"* I'm not trying to be rude, but sometimes I just want to carry on with my day without having to spit bars about my identity to someone who I'll never even meet again. Sometimes I just want to sit quietly and not get asked questions in front of others and feel like I am being singled out as "that foreign kid" in class. Surely, it's never the intention of the professors asking those questions, but the truth is some people just view and treat you differently when they know you're "not from here."

DO YOU HAVE AN ENGLISH NAME?

There were many times where instead of putting in the effort to know my name, people asked me for an English name instead. The first time it happened to me was during the first week of arriving in Los Angeles. I was on the phone making a dinner reservation and after having to spell out my name letter by letter to the lady over the phone—who kept messing it up—she asked, "Do you have another name you go by?" I told her no and resorted to reciting names of miscellaneous objects with initials that spell out my name until she finally got it right. On another occasion that same year, I was at an office on campus getting some paperwork done and the man working at the front desk messed up the spelling of my name the first time I said it to him. He then said, "Just give me your English name," and when I told him I didn't have one, he let out an exasperated sigh with an annoyed look on his face while hitting the backspace button on his keyboard a few times, then he asked me to start over again.

Perhaps it's pathetic but I came home that evening and, of all the things stressing me out in my life at that time, that was *the thing* to make me burst into tears for three minutes in my dorm room. Something about that situation made me remember a time back in high school when a teacher said to me, *"If you had an English name, you look like you could be a Cindy,"* and so ever since then, I decided to adopt *Cindy* as my fake English name. Don't get me wrong, friends, professors, and other people I frequently interact with all still referred to me as *Indah*. It was everyone else outside of that group I introduced myself as Cindy to—Uber, Lyft, Starbucks. Initially it was pretty weird, and my friends and I would sometimes laugh at it a little, but I enjoyed the convenience it granted me in a lot of situations. Most people didn't stop to ask me questions whenever I told them I was *Cindy*. Sometimes it even felt like they didn't stare at me as much to try and figure out where the name might be from, as they normally would with a name like *Indah*.

* * *

I lived in a dorm with a Vietnamese American roommate during my freshman year. I remember one night, not too long after just moving in and getting to know her, I had asked her how to pronounce her Vietnamese name. While on that topic, she told me she thought my name was really pretty, and I thanked her. She then jokingly asked me if I was cool with her calling me *Indie* as a nickname because she thought it was cute and it rhymed a little more with her name. I knew it was just a joke and she meant absolutely no harm by saying it, but the more I thought about it, the more I wondered whether her joke was actually symptomatic of a much bigger societal problem.

See, I can't think of anywhere else in the world, outside of the anglosphere, where it is considered respectful—let alone *normal*—to casually ask people you barely know or have a special relationship with to go by a completely different name in a completely different language just because it's more convenient for you. In the Chinese language, they have direct translations of English names, so even if they call you *Da Wei* instead of *David*, they're still accommodating to the same name, just in a different language. In Indonesia, people may pronounce your name as *Trisya* instead of *Trisha*, but they're still the same name, just in a different pronunciation.

In English-speaking cultures, if your name is *Xin Yu*, people expect you to go by *Sarah*. If your name is *Channarong*, they want you to go by *Jake*. There have been multiple occasions where people have even *suggested* I use an English name—and it wasn't that they were trying to be rude, they were actually looking out for my best interest. Their argument was always it would be better *for my sake*. It would give me a better chance of getting recruited; it would help avoid mispronunciations and misspellings, which would help me be taken more seriously by others. A professor even once told me it would help me seem more approachable to the other students in class.

Every time I picked up my resume and saw my name written on top in big bold letters, I liked to imagine scenarios in my head of what an American recruiter would think when looking at it. Would they be intrigued by it enough to actually look at my resume for more than five seconds? Or would they immediately chuck it aside because they're not sure if someone with a name like mine would even know how to speak English? People are aware of racial bias, gender bias, even discrimination on the basis of sexuality, religion, and political affiliation in the workforce, but very rarely do we discuss name bias—and this is especially pervasive in the West.

According to the US National Bureau of Economic Research, applicants with white-sounding names received far more callbacks for interviews compared to applicants with Black-sounding names by a staggering 50 percent.[2] Research from the University of Toronto and Ryerson University revealed when thirteen thousand fake resumes were sent out

---

2   Bertrand Marianne and Sendhil Mullainathan, "Are Emily and Greg More Employable than Lakisha and Jamal? A Field Experiment on Labor Market Discrimination," *The American Economic Review* Vol. 94, No. 4 (2004): 991.

to 3,225 job vacancies in Toronto and Montreal, candidates with Asian last names were 28 percent less likely to make the interview stage compared to other candidates with English names, even though they all had the exact same qualifications and experience levels.[3] Despite equality legislations and anti-discrimination laws, people like me still have to wonder every time we've been rejected, or don't hear back from a job application, if it is because we were under qualified or because we were just born with the wrong name.

In high school, all the international students needed to adopt an acceptable American name, supposedly to assimilate better into American culture. Currently in the US, I'm discouraged to put my legal name on things such as my resume or my LinkedIn profile because it would serve as a disadvantage during my job search.

—RACHEL CAI | HONG KONG

It is especially hard when I am applying for jobs. I already put on a fake "white" accent during job interviews, as if it would provide some sort of leverage. Whenever I'm interested in a guy from Canada who may be Caucasian, I fear telling them my name because it is always followed by "Where are you from?" I sometimes feel uncomfortable telling them my nationality as I feel it may make me look less desirable.

—ANONYMOUS | GHANA

---

3   Rupa Banerjee, Jeffrey G. Reitz, and Phil Oreopoulos, "Do Large Employers Treat Racial Minorities More Fairly? An Analysis of Canadian Field Experiment Data," *Canadian Public Policy / Analyse De Politiques* Vol. 44, No. 1 (2018): 2.

* * *

One day while I was venting to a friend about all of this, they asked, "So, why don't you just use the name Cindy more often if it makes your life so much easier? People use nicknames and aliases all the time, and they don't have to know it's fake." On the one hand, that is true. One of the first friends I met during international orientation was a girl from Botswana. She first introduced herself to me as *Tapiwa*, and then about a year after, I was surprised to find out she had started going by the name *Karen*. I don't think there's anything wrong with wanting to adopt a different name, whether it's for the sake of convenience or just wanting to reinvent an entirely new identity from scratch. The problem for me was I had already gone through all of that when I went from *Putri* to *Indah*. I had to make a habit out of introducing myself with a different name and explain to the people who knew me by my old name why I was suddenly going by a new name, on top of the amount of time it took for other people, *and myself,* to finally start feeling comfortable with that new identity.

I didn't want to go through the whole process all over again the second time. It was unfair to me, *and for what? Because people can't learn to do the bare minimum and say someone's name correctly?* I don't regret the names I've been given at birth, nor do I regret the way people have disrespected them throughout my childhood. My only regret is I allowed them to, so much so I started doing it to myself. Our names are not just characterizations of our ethnicity or nationality, but also of who and what we are at the very essence of our existence. They shouldn't be a tax we have to pay just to be treated with basic human decency, but I had already paid mine just to be able to survive at an English-speaking school, and I wasn't about to pay it the second time just to be able to live in an English-speaking country.

That old name was tied to my old self, who was okay, but there's so much of that person I worked so hard to change. So, just like how some people cut their hair or do something else as equally dramatic, taking on a new name (which luckily was already one of my three official names in my passport) symbolized evolution for me.

—KAREN TAFA | BOTSWANA

IT'S REALLY NOT THAT HARD

Did you know Rihanna is actually pronounced like *Ree-Anna,* or that it's Ariana *Gran-Dee, not Gran-Day?* Lucy *Liu* is pronounced *Lee-Yoo* not *Loo.* Chrissy *Teigen* is pronounced *Tai-Ghen.* Jake Gyllenhaal's last name is actually pronounced *Yee-Len-Hey-Lo.* We even butcher countries and cities. Qatar is pronounced like "cutter" in English. Hawaii is *Huh-Va-Ee.* It's *Co-LOM-Bia,* not *Co-Lum-Bee-Ya,* and the capital city of Thailand is pronounced *Bahng-Gawk.* At school, we've all had to learn how to pronounce names like Caesar, Van Gogh, Charlemagne, and Chopin correctly, but most people don't know how to properly pronounce Mao Ze Dong or Gandhi. Even in mainstream culture today, most English speakers know how to say names like Kyle, Genevieve, Hugh, Eleanor, and Lincoln, but not Hernandez, Nguyen, Zhang, or Chopra.

I don't feel comfortable giving myself an English name just because some people cannot pronounce my real name. I have always been called by my real name for years, and don't want to go by some other name just because I moved to the United States.

—SHUBHECHHA DHAR | INDIA

My point is, it's really not hard to get someone's name right if you have some level of basic human decency to put in the time and effort to remember it. *Don't be an asshole.* It's not funny when you butcher someone's name, either accidentally or purposefully, or blatantly mock the way it looks or sounds altogether. It's not your place to interrogate anybody about whether or not that's really how their names are supposed to be pronounced or spelled, nor do you have authority over how someone's name should sound, look, or even be. *Also, for God's sake, stop saying stupid shit like:* "No, that can't be your real name." "Wow, your name is so exotic." "Is that your *real* name?" "Do you have an easier name you go by?" "Can I call you [insert something that is not your name] instead?" *No, you can't.* **If you can learn to say supercalifragilisticexpialidocious, then I think you can learn to say someone's fucking name.**

When I was about to start college, my older brother asked me what name I was going to go by in America, and I explained I had made the choice to go by my given name. It was a weird moment where we were both explicitly aware of the shared experience of having to make ourselves accessible to the anglophone world, and it was understood that going by my own name was a small form of protest.

—WONG YU WEN | MALAYSIA & SINGAPORE

In Nepali and Hindu tradition, a couple months after you are born, you go through a naming ceremony and your name or first initial is dependent on your time, date of birth, and the stars. My name means moonlight, and I have always looked at the moon for solace in times of difficulty.

—ANONYMOUS | NEPAL & KENYA

In class, I immediately know when I have come up on the roster because the professors always pause and scrunch their faces a little. It's a response I've become used to looking for. I am always ready to tell them I have a second name that is easier to go by.

—NAUKALEMO GLORIA DEL MAR NDILULA | NAMIBIA

I was called TV instead of Tanvi by my PE teacher when she called out the register, and my friends used to mock me for it (all in good fun). I've also had people call me "Tammy" or "Tanbi" or "Tandi." It's annoying quite a lot of the time because I'll be meeting new people, many times in a group, and others will usually have a "regular" name like "Sam," and then it will get to me, and I'll have to repeat my name a few times and also see the look of stress on the person's face as they now have to remember a "weird" name.

—TANVI WADHWA | UNITED KINGDOM & INDIA

You could be uneducated and have an English name and people would view you as intelligent, whereas you could hold multiple degrees and be incredibly intelligent and people would still look down on you because of your non-English name.

—DAISY INGREY | UNITED KINGDOM

I feel like I am called on less in class because of my non-English name, and people are uncomfortable with not being able to assume my gender from looking at it.

—ZI YI LIM | SINGAPORE

I had a professor adopt an English name to use versus her Korean name because a lot of students wanted an "American" teaching them American history. She was, in fact, American born and raised, but her name is of South Korean origins.

—THENNY WIDJAJA | INDONESIA

I had a friend who told me, due to his Muslim name, he often gets rejected for job interviews. He said this is why he always requests a phone interview, so the people on the other line can understand he speaks English well and doesn't uphold their racist expectations. I think about that a lot because it was the first time it really came to my attention that even names are racially coded within our employment system.

—REBECCA SANGS | CAMBODIA, GERMANY, UNITED ARAB EMIRATES, INDONESIA, & CHINA

A friend once told me, "Thank God you have an English name, or we wouldn't have been friends if I couldn't pronounce your name.

—MELISSA KWAN | SINGAPORE

English names are considered cool and more international, as opposed to traditional names that are considered more old-fashioned. It can also be assumed that society has an inferiority complex due to the effect of Western colonization, creating a psychological scar and mindset that they are worth less than the colony, and thus need the affirmation and appreciation from other more prosperous countries. Using English names is one way to get that attention.

—ANONYMOUS | INDONESIA

I would not want my kids to legally inherit my Chinese surname. I want my kids to have the privilege of being able to pass in a white society so they could open doors and opportunities I may have never even been considered for, and if that means giving up a piece of their name and their heritage, I would do it.

—ANONYMOUS | UNITED STATES

In most of my classes where I'm the only international student, I get a lot of anxiety when I have to speak in front of the entire class because I know they're not paying attention to what I say, but to how I sound.

—MADHURI THACKERAY | INDIA

.

CHAPTER 2

"OH, YOUR ENGLISH IS SO GOOD!"

GOOD ENGLISH

For the life of me, I will never understand why so many people from English-speaking countries seem to have such a fascination with foreigners being able to speak their language. Almost all international students have either seen this happen to someone we know or experienced this for ourselves at least once: They would probe us on how and why we "speak English so fluently," and then maybe, if we're so lucky enough, they would even compliment us on how our "English is so good!" You get extra points if "You don't even have an accent!" *It's almost as if people forget the British invaded almost 90 percent of the world.[4] Over 1.2 billion people (20 percent of the world) today speak English.[5]*

---

4   Stuart Laycock, *All the Countries We've Ever Invaded: And the Few We Never Got Round To* (Cheltenham: History Press, 2012).

5   "The Most Spoken Languages Worldwide in 2019," Statista, Publication November 27, 2020.

However annoying these questions and comments are, I do see the validity of their curiosity as well. Indonesia is not an English-speaking country. On the English Proficiency Index by English First (EF), the world's largest ranking of English skills by country, Indonesia ranks thirty-second out of seventy-two countries surveyed, lower than most of its regional peers in Southeast Asia.[6] Even people from Indonesia would often get shocked when they learn that English is actually my first language. Mandarin Chinese was my second language, as required by school, and although I was born and raised in Indonesia, Indonesian was actually the third language I learned.

It comes from ignorance regarding how colonization (in the past and presently) works, why we were made to learn English growing up in schools, how the language even got to our local schools, and why it's made mandatory. Both my parents grew up without English as their first languages, if spoken at all at home. When they had children, they decided raising my siblings and I with English as our first language would benefit us greatly when we got older, the same reason as to why they gave us English names.

—ALYSSA CHUA JIA YU | MALAYSIA

The lack of Indonesian education at school and my mother's frequent absence from home greatly impacted my language skills growing up. It wasn't until twelfth grade when I made my first Indonesian friend who I could actually practice conversing in Indonesian with that I started improving. All

---

6   "Communicating Across Borders: How Well Do Indonesians Speak English?," *Indonesia Investments*, August 7, 2017.

my life up until that point, I struggled to even go out and about *in my own city*. It was even hard at home. I feel like a lot of the misunderstandings my mother and I had during my earlier years growing up were largely due to the fact we had a large language barrier. English was my most fluent language, but it wasn't hers. Communicating with parents in general is already a struggle in and of itself. It's an *absolute fucking nightmare* when the both of you don't even share the same primary languages or are at entirely opposite proficiency levels.

I didn't know how to speak up and stand up for myself whenever I got in trouble for things I felt I shouldn't have been punished for. I didn't know how to communicate whenever she asked me what I wanted to do when I grew up. I didn't know how to share my thoughts and opinions on certain things. I couldn't give her a coherent answer as to why I was sad or angry. I didn't know how to explain to her why I hated school, why I got into fights with some of the other kids, or why I was failing some of my classes. It wasn't that I lacked the emotional capacity to talk about all these things, it's that I lacked the language capacity to talk with her. I think there were times my mother did try to understand where I was coming from, but of course it was hard for her when the very thing I was always struggling with was how to translate my struggles to her in the first place.

I had spent my entire life feeling like I didn't belong in my own home because I only knew how to speak English in a non-English-speaking country. When I finally moved to an English-speaking country and was surrounded by other fluent English speakers just like me, I was hit with the dilemma of people using my skin color and nationality as a starting point in forming preconceived notions about me and my linguistic abilities.

＊ ＊ ＊

In one of my freshman elective classes, a professor told me, "You might want to consider seeking resources on campus to help with your English for this essay." The comment felt out of line because I had never expressed needing help with my English in the first place. I had never even talked to this professor about who I was and where I was from because it was only the first week of classes. I'm guessing he had simply assumed—from my name— I was a foreigner, and therefore spoke poor English. "Oh, how funny," I thought, because most of the time people just assume based on my accent I'm a born and raised American, only to then be surprised by the fact I actually speak English well despite coming from Indonesia (as if those two conditions are somehow mutually exclusive).

I had a new English teacher, and upon reading my writing for the first time, he accused me of plagiarism because he doubted I was capable of writing in such a sophisticated manner. It was as humiliating as it was infuriating when he then submitted my essay into a plagiarism website trying to prove it wasn't my original work, only to then be shocked to discover it actually was.

—SARITA CRUZ | HONDURAS

I have a friend from back in college named Max, a white boy from Germany. In freshman year, while we were both still living in the same dorm building, we would sometimes go grocery shopping together. On one of those occasions, during the Uber ride back to campus the driver asked the both of us where we were from, to which we told her I was from Jakarta and he was from Berlin. The driver asked us questions about if we were university students and if we had recently moved to LA, but then she turned *to me* and asked, "How'd you learn English so quick?" It was interesting the driver had only asked *me* that question, and not Max, even though Max is the one who speaks English as a second language with a perceptible German accent.

People start making comments about my English once they find out where I'm from. Before that, the way I speak never seems to cross their mind.

—ANONYMOUS | FINLAND

One day this lady asked me where I was from, and I just gave her the short and easy answer, and I told her I was from Los Angeles. She looked at me, confused. I added I was born in Hong Kong, and she immediately said, "Wow, your English is great." I already told her I was from LA, so she clearly already had assumptions prior to asking questions.

—SELENA RUIZI YIN | HONG KONG, UNITED
STATES, UNITED KINGDOM, & CHINA

Of course, many of these people simply do not know any better. They do not have any malicious intentions in saying these things, but while these types of remarks are microaggressions that are annoying on the surface, the underlying implications shed light on a bigger and more harmful systemic flaw. *Why would these people think these things about us, unless they already had presumptions we would not be able to speak English well in the first place?* You might be wondering what's the big deal if some people think you may not be able to speak a certain language. English isn't just *any* language, and English at its core isn't *just* a language either.

THE INTIMIDATION OF ENGLISH

For as long as I have been cognizant of my accent as a child, I have always sounded—to quote everybody and their mothers—"very white." I received this comment so much growing up in Indonesia (or while traveling) that strangers thought I was either half-white or from the US. For most people outside of the anglosphere, speaking in English has always meant speaking like an American. I've thought about how funny this is considering the authentic English accent is the British accent because the language originates from Britain.

The proliferation of America's influence over recent decades—whether it be through the prominence of Hollywood in global media and entertainment, or other international relations such as politics—is the obvious and simplified answer as to why many foreigners like me tend to pick up American accents when speaking English abroad. Personally, this was further reinforced by my enrollment in an American institution during high school.

After moving to the States, people often questioned the authenticity of my American accent. They would ask if I adopted it to mask my "real" one. A professor once asked me if I used to have "a more Asian accent" before coming to America. What was even more common was friends, professors, and even random strangers complimenting me for how I "don't even have an accent." *Yes, I do, I have an American accent.* Some international students I've met don't even have any particular accent, instead they have more of an *international dialect.* The way I describe this is their English—be it through their accent, intonations, or other aspects of their language—is *unmarked*, ambiguous, and not really belonging to any particular location. It's not necessarily American, or British, or Canadian, or Australian, or Kiwi, but it's also not necessarily the local accent of wherever region they are from either. It was always so interesting to me how many of the Americans I met had the tendency to think their accent is the universal standard. To be "accented" meant not speaking in an American accent, which was often perceived to be either weird or wrong. I talk a lot about accents in this chapter because it dictates so much more than we often give it credit for.

Speaking English can be an intimidating experience for those who either didn't have access to quality English education, started learning English at a later age, or were never in an environment where they could frequently practice speaking the language. Sometimes this means their understanding of grammar and their spelling abilities aren't as strong, or the breadth of their English lexicon isn't as wide. What I've found was even for those who have perfect grammar and spelling, or even a much more extensive English vocabulary than average, all of these are often weighed down if they "speak with an accent."

It varies; for some, that accent is more audible and consistent throughout their speech, while others have developed masking abilities where you'd only occasionally catch them slipping back into their original accents. When my friend Jenna Nguyen and I rushed for a business fraternity at LMU, we found out from a friend, who was already a brother in that fraternity, the reason why they rejected her was because they said her English wasn't good enough. Speaking as a friend, and from an objective point of view, Jenna's English comprehension and command of grammatical structure and lexis were fine. If anything, considering how she started learning English at the age of eleven through being forced by her dad to highlight and memorize words in English newspapers, her linguistic skills were nothing short of amazing. The only thing was she spoke with an audibly Vietnamese accent that, although it did not impact much of her speech, the fraternity seemed to take issue with it anyway.

The fault of the English education in Indonesia is it focuses more on articulation than comprehension. They don't care that the students don't understand what is being discussed, the spelling is wrong, or the grammar is all messed up as much as they care about being able to just sound good while speaking. In local Indonesian schools, the way teachers train their students for this is to put students on the spot and have them get up in front of the room to either read a passage or answer questions in English. If the students got criticized or penalized for a mistake they made, it was done in front of the whole class to watch and judge, and it's traumatizing. It's no wonder so many Indonesians then grow up intimidated to speak in English and are even intimidated by people like me who speak English well. The entirety of their English education has been built upon the foundations of fear and humiliation.

Somehow, in Asia English has been made into a premium product instead of a utility product. People focus more on sounding native because of the prestige attached to the language when really the focus should be more on using it as a utility. Can you listen? Can you understand? Can you talk, and can they understand? Your accent shouldn't matter.

—MIKAEL HARSENO SUBIANTO | INDONESIA

English, as a language, is intimidating largely because of the power that has been associated with it throughout time. It has been the most powerful language in the world for more than a century. *For fuck's sake, it was the language of most of our oppressors.* It's the dominant language of three G7 nations (US, UK, and Canada), not to mention the British colonist legacy has surely attributed to its widespread global footprint. I would argue the global dominance of the US and the UK throughout history has also been, in some part, due to their English proficiency. According to the Oxford Dictionary, English has the most expansive vocabulary of any language in the world, providing an extremely rich arsenal of expressions the size of which is unprecedented in human history. English has been used as a potent tool for figures, like Shakespeare and Bill Gates, to change the world.[7]

English has never been just a language to the rest of the world. English has always been a status, a ranking; it was always made to be a symbol of your class, your intellect, and your worth. The British empire had such a strong, pervasive influence that their language continued to dominate the world even decades following their collapse. In tandem with the influence of language was the influence of white supremacy. The British invaded almost every country in the world, and people needed to know English not just because they belonged to the British, but because knowing English also made them better than those who didn't. Parents in other countries today invest however much money they need to, or are able to afford, into their children's English education. They do this by either enrolling them in an English-based

---

7   Eva Du Monteil, "Which Language Has the Most Words?," *Babbel Magazine,* February 1, 2020.

school or signing them up at English tutoring facilities outside of school.

They feel the need to go to this extent because they know the ability to speak English on an almost—if not entirely—native level will grant their kids access to opportunities and privileges not made available to those who can't use the language. This is true whether it's in the anglosphere or outside of it. Your ability to speak English will often mean the difference as to whether or not *you* get chosen for that job over someone else who shares all of the same qualities, credentials, and work experiences as you. In many countries like Indonesia, there is a level of prestige immediately attached onto other people's perception of you the moment they know you can speak English. To them it means you have been able to afford studying abroad or had the luxury of attending an international school in the country. In terms of your skills, aptitude, and even wealth, you could be on the exact same level as someone else, but both of you are going to be judged differently depending on who speaks better English.

When people hear I'm from Hong Kong, but I look Indian, and I speak German, they are confused as to why my "English is so good" without realizing it's my mother-tongue. When I moved to England, the microaggression of not looking like I had a high understanding of English felt like a slap in the face. The assumption was often I couldn't possibly be as well-spoken as them if I didn't grow up in a country that had English as a native language.

—SOPHIE BURKHARDT | HONG KONG

I was doing a recital in Korea over the summer a few years ago, and it was basically a lucky draw for performers who applied for the spot. They picked me because I was the only candidate who had both a respectable and notable education and had English in my performing resume. I was selected not for my performance ability, but based on the fact my whole resume was in English rather than Korean, so the performance venue can have the chance to say, "We have someone who is Western educated performing at our hall."

—ANONYMOUS | SOUTH KOREA & INDONESIA

As foreigners from non-anglophone countries, it's always been ingrained in us that we can't afford to make a mistake when speaking in English. Whether it has been indoctrinated through an institution or by lived experience, we have been trained to be conscious—for some even *hyperconscious*—of making even the slightest grammatical or vocabulary mistake, of slipping into "an accent," or of mispronouncing just about anything. During one occurrence where I had forgotten how to say something in English, the person I was talking to laughed and said, "No, you're good, English is hard. I get it." I'm sure they meant no offense, but to me, it was like a slap in the face. Suddenly it felt like all the hard work I had put into all the other times I demonstrated how eloquent and competent I was in speaking in an educated and refined manner was immediately discredited because of one tiny blunder. Whenever my American classmates made a mistake, people made it seem attributable to nothing more than mere human error—*we're all human, we all make mistakes, we forget things*—but whenever I made a mistake, I felt like people often attributed it to the fact I was a foreigner.

COMPROMISE

Jakarta has a significant number of Western expats (mainly Americans and Australians) who came to live for work-related purposes. Many of them included my teachers at school. My friends and I would notice how most of them did not know how to speak Bahasa Indonesia, despite having lived there for many years. They would go about their everyday lives interacting with the locals speaking in English, and I was never sure if it was because they were too shy to speak or just never bothered learning. Even when they would end up residing permanently in Indonesia to start a family, regardless of the culture they're marrying into, they often spoke to their Indonesian spouses in English.

Meanwhile, stories of microaggressions and harassments in the anglosphere toward people speaking in their own languages other than English are not uncommon to read on the news or hear from personal anecdotes, as I have had to experience myself. When I went with my mother to a nearby Rite Aid to buy a few things, she was trying to communicate with one of the store workers but gave up midway because she didn't know how to proceed with her sentence in English. She turned to me to translate for her. In the middle of my mother explaining to me what it was she was looking for, the store worker standing right in front of the both of us said to me in an annoyed tone, "Can't she just speak to me in English?" *If my mother knew how to say it in English, what makes you think she wouldn't?*

The same people who travel abroad and complain nobody else speaks English are the same people who attack immigrants, tourists, and even their own naturalized citizens for speaking in their own languages within their own groups. When we speak bad English, we're often made to apologize.

We get told to either learn English or go back to where we came from by the same people who come to *our countries* barely speaking our language, and yet somehow they feel entitled to be welcomed with open arms.

Societies around the world have placed English so high up on the linguistic pedestal, in part due to institutions that have taught generations of young students to internalize the exact same mindset. An Indian friend told me students at their school were often punished into writing "I will never speak Hindi while in school" about a hundred times on the board during detention. When I was in middle school, I was getting scolded for code-switching between English, Indonesian, and Mandarin with some of my classmates. Rules were enforced to ensure students only spoke in proper English while on campus grounds. The administrators were afraid of how groups of students speaking *any other languages* would impact their attractiveness as a school that was supposed to educate some of the brightest and smartest kids in the country.

I wish I would have learned more about the Indonesian language instead of pushing it away because of my language disability and the difficulty. I wished I had provided the same amount of attention to Indonesian as I did to English. In my elementary school, policies that completely banned students from communicating with one another in Indonesian prevented me from improving, and often times I had to pretend I either understood or pretend I didn't speak Indonesian at all.

—GRACE SUTANTO | INDONESIA

Faculties at university institutions that pride themselves on their diversity and mission toward social justice are no exception. At LMU, I had a professor who, after complimenting me for my articulate English abilities, proceeded to reprimand other international students for, according to them, "not speaking enough English when they're in an American university." In 2019, the head of the Masters of Biostatistics program at Duke University sent out an email to warn students against not speaking in English in a professional setting after she had been approached by two faculty members who complained about international students speaking Chinese in student lounge and study areas.[8]

It is unfortunate we are living in a time where educators are actively discouraging multilingualism in fear it either undermines our English abilities or diminishes the quality or prestige of a certain space. In reality, English is often prioritized so much more than other languages, especially within the professional and academia world, that we compromise more than just our knowledge and skills in our mother tongues, we sacrifice culture for the sake of esteem. These days, in spaces where English demands to be given special attention, speaking another language is often seen as an act of rebellion.

8   Harmeet Kaur, "A Duke professor warned Chinese students to speak English," *CNN*, January 29, 2019.

I think the more I gravitated toward speaking English, the more I also gravitated toward English culture. Internalized racism and being surrounded by the English language made me grow up distancing myself from Mandarin, and in turn, my primary language skills have decreased significantly. Now, I regret not appreciating my native language more.

—AMY LIU YUE YANG | CHINA & CANADA

This has happened a lot in the UK where people would "dumb-down" their English while talking to me. It was strange because I would speak back in perfect English. It was just very confusing to me when people did that because, in my opinion, they would be lowering their chances of having a more meaningful conversation with someone else.

—JABRIEL ALSUHAIMI | SINGAPORE & SAUDI ARABIA

In Japan, there is a very weird and harmful culture where "kikokushijo" (returnee kids) from English-speaking countries are often regarded as people who are too westernized, who think they are cool for speaking in English, and who think they are above other Japanese people who have only lived in Japan their whole lives. I avoid mixing English when I speak Japanese because I want to prove I can speak Japanese properly even though I am a "kikokushijo." Sometimes I end up having to mix in English when I cannot remember the Japanese word for what I want to say, or when I want to talk about an idea that simply cannot be translated into Japanese.

—MAI MIURA | JAPAN

When I go up to someone, I know what I want to ask, and I know what I need, but when they start talking, my mind immediately goes blank, and I panic a bit on the inside. It's a big insecurity of mine, knowing my English isn't that great, and other Asian kids are able to speak in an American accent, but I can't.

—FELICIA AGNES | INDONESIA

I really do not like other people making assumptions about my English when they don't even speak a second language, and I speak three.

—KARLA SOFIA MEDINA ROMERO | DOMINICAN REPUBLIC

People from English-speaking countries tend to not learn other languages because they know most of the world speaks theirs, so why would they?

—PAULA GARBIN | CROATIA

Proficiency in use of language conversationally usually does not pay as much attention to accents. Having gone to university in the UK, I feel as though most native speakers expect the non-native-speaking students to have a higher level of English proficiency, given it's often a requirement to be able to study here.

—ANONYMOUS | NORWAY

I remember clearly one incident that hurt me the most was when I was on a taxi ride back from the airport to my apartment, and the taxi driver said to me, "I know you're not from Australia. Your English has a weird accent. I knew you weren't fluent."

—ANONYMOUS | INDONESIA

It sucks whenever I come back home. I remember having these memories of playing with my cousins, singing with my grandparents, and running around with my aunts and uncles. I can't have those memories anymore because I just can't speak to them comfortably. During family dinners, sometimes my cousins will try and avoid talking to me. I do the same because I am embarrassed. The loss of my Indonesian tongue has always been something I am ashamed of.

—IDA AYU SAKIRA HERMAWAN |
SAUDI ARABIA & INDONESIA

Speaking English as a second language can be utilized to make an awesome first impression. If they are expecting bad or mediocre English, you can just dazzle them with good English, and create an everlasting first impression.

—NAGA ABHILASH CHADARAM | INDIA

I never really felt like I had a home growing up because we moved so often, and I got really good at packing my suitcases. Home for me was more of the few token personal belongings that went with me from place to place—like a doll or a photo album—as well as my immediate family members—a very small nuclear family with my mom, my dad, my brother, and myself. It wasn't until I was in graduate school, and I visited Illinois for the first time, that I felt like I was home the minute I showed up. People there were very welcoming, and it didn't matter where I was from or where I'd lived. As long as I wanted to put my roots down there in Illinois, I was from Illinois. My parents or grandparents didn't have to live there or be from there. Home then became a place that was accepting of me and all of the different parts of who I was.

—US SENATOR OF ILLINOIS TAMMY DUCKWORTH
| THAILAND, CAMBODIA, INDONESIA,
SINGAPORE, & UNITED STATES

CHAPTER 3

THE FAULT IN
THE COOKIE CUTTER

Featuring US Senator of Illinois
Tammy Duckworth

INTRODUCING ME

Where are you from? Where is home? Some of us can give one-word, one-second answers, while others need one whole minute—or a whole chapter, in my case—to explain this often intricate part of our identities. Most kids with international or multicultural backgrounds have cookie-cutter answers to where we're from—a quick one-city or one-country response that never fully and accurately paints the whole picture of who we are and why, but it suffices. People often use where in the world we're physically or ethnically from as a way to gauge what kind of life we've lived or what sort of experiences we belong to, but when we're restricted to cookie-cutter answers, we leave behind the other bits and pieces of the dough.

I was born in Thailand, I lived in Cambodia, Indonesia, and Singapore. I bounced back and forth between Indonesia, Thailand, and Singapore for quite a while, and it was mainly Singapore and Thailand I hopped between a lot. I lived in Jakarta for seven years, which was the longest I had ever lived anywhere in my early life, so Indonesia in many ways was home for me. My dad moved between jobs a lot, so we would just go to wherever the job took us.

—TAMMY DUCKWORTH

I have never lived anywhere more than five years, so usually I would just claim my passport nation which is the US.

—CHANDLER COOPER | UNITED
STATES, THAILAND, & CHINA

At this point in the book, you know before moving to LA I lived in Jakarta, Indonesia and was born and raised there my entire life. My mother's side of the family is from Southern China, so that makes us Chinese Indonesians. Indonesia is a very diverse country and is one of the most ethnically diverse societies in the world, consisting of roughly 1,300 different ethnic groups with at least 95 percent belonging to native Indonesian ancestry. Minority migrant groups such as the Chinese, like myself, the Arabs, and the Indians make up the remainder.[9] *Oh, and most of us are at least partially ethnically mixed with one another.* If you were to look up "What do Indonesians look like?" on Google, you'd find

---

9   Sarah Yuniarni, "Unity in Diversity: Indonesia's Six Largest Ethnic Groups," *Jakarta Globe*, July 16, 2016.

everything from different physical characteristics, religious backgrounds, cultural styles, diverse foods, some Barack Obama photos, and my personal favorite, a Quora post from July 17, 2020 with the title *"Why do Indonesian People Look Half-Asian and Half-African?"*[10]

I've always struggled with the question "Where are you from?" because I always had many different versions of answers that I never knew either where to start or what people were looking for. Were they asking where I'm *ethnically* from, *nationally* from, or where *the experiences that have made me* were from? Whenever I'd tell people I'm *from Indonesia*, most would often respond *"but you look Chinese,"* or Japanese, or Thai, or literally insert any other mainstream Asian ethnicity that matches the image of a pair of slanted eyes and fair skin. Then they'd get confused when I told them I *am* Chinese, and would say "But you just said you're from Indonesia?" On the other hand, when I bring up my Chinese heritage to kids I'd meet from China, Taiwan, or Hong Kong as a way to establish common ground on the basis of similar culture, sometimes they'd tell me "You don't look Chinese," followed by comments like "You look more Filipino or Vietnamese." Then they would get confused when I tell them I'm *from* Indonesia, and say "But you just said you're Chinese?"

Whenever I limit my answer to just "Bolivia," I tend to get more questions as to why I speak perfect English or Italian, or how I ended up in London, and so on. So many times, I end up having to tell a little chunk of my story. I've had people find

---

10   "Why Do Indonesian People Look Like Half-Asian and Half-African?," *Quora*, Published July 17, 2020.

it super cool and interesting, and they wanted to hear more about my culture, the different countries I've lived in, and so on. Of course, I've also had annoying questions like "Do you guys have TV in Bolivia?" or "Why are you white?"

—RAQUEL CHAVEZ CORS | BOLIVIA, ITALY, VENEZUELA, & CHILE

I always have to take the extra time and effort to explain to people *by ethnicity* I'm Chinese because that's where my ancestry is from, but *by nationality* I'm Indonesian because I was born and raised there. Sometimes that ends up confusing people even more. I feel like a lot of people, especially those from more ethnically homogenous societies, still have generally poor basic understandings of the differences between ethnicity, nationality, and even sometimes race. Slightly off topic, but here is a funny story: I was at the DMV in LA, and this young woman in her twenties next to me asked me, "Are you Chinese, or are you Asian?" I looked at her confused and responded, "Chinese *is* Asian," and she said, "No, no, I mean, like, are you from China, or are you from, like, an Asian country?" Let that sink in.

BIG FOREIGNER ENERGY

Growing up at international schools, all of my closest friends were Koreans, Japanese, Indians, Malaysians, Australians, Americans, Filipinos, and tons of other kids from other nationalities who made up the expat community in Jakarta. Indonesian citizens like myself made up the minority of the student population at the schools I attended. I felt I didn't even really have a specific culture I identified with because of the culmination of being raised in a westernized educational environment and coming from an already mixed-culture family background. My sense of culture has just always largely been an accumulation of all the different customs and traditions from all over the world I grew up exposed to from school.

Sometimes it really gets to me when people talk about "back home" and "hometown friends" because I know for a fact I can't relate. I usually feel homesick for a place, but I'm not even sure where.

—ECEM GIDERGI | TURKEY, CHINA, & INDONESIA

I didn't feel *entirely* Chinese, or *entirely* Indonesian, either. Chinese Indonesians, as a collective of immigrants, are always too Chinese for the Indonesians but too Indonesian for the Chinese. That's why we form our own distinct mixed-ethnic group (usually shortened to "*Chindos*") to create a new space to exist between both cultures—*and yet I still don't fit in there.* The lack of exposure to Chinese Indonesian society as a kid has made me struggle to establish enough common ground and create meaningful relationships whenever I do try reaching out to them. The other issue besides language was also barely—if any—of the cultural norms, outlooks, and values shared by most Chinese Indonesians ever resonated with me. I always felt more western-oriented, even though Western culture was neither something I could fully identify with, nor claim as my own even if I had wanted to. I was always too western for the East, but too eastern for the West. I never qualified as just Chinese, I never qualified as just Indonesian, and suddenly I couldn't even qualify for both, either.

I always felt like I could never get away with just giving one answer because I feel like I'm picking one culture in betrayal of the other. Where's the line between wanting to fully acknowledge and embrace the entirety of my identity, but also wanting to avoid rambling about a question most people, in most situations, just want a cookie-cutter answer to?

"So, are you more Chinese, or are you more Indonesian?"

"Oh, so you're not that Chinese then."

"Oh, so you're not really Indonesian then."

What the fuck is that even supposed to mean? How do you even measure that? If it wasn't about how I looked, it was always about how I sounded. The immediate assumption was always I couldn't have had such a strong American accent without having been raised, or at least having lived for some period of time, in America. In reality, I've had an American accent even before moving to the US. I don't get why even to this day people are so surprised by that when literally the overwhelming majority of online English audio content all around the world is provided in the standard American accent.

The other aspect about going to an international school is we lived in a bubble. Perhaps this wasn't an issue for the expat kids who were only going to live in Indonesia for a short term, but it hits different when you're a local like me. Not only was I born and raised there, but I also had the intentions of pursuing a permanent life and career there even after being done with school. When you're young, you don't know how to compartmentalize your life at school with your friends from your life at home with your family, or even from your life with other people outside of both. Going to an American high school in Jakarta sort of felt like living in a miniature appropriated version of America, only to then be stunned by the reality of how different my life at home, as well as outside of home, actually was beyond the gated walls of campus. I was never taught social knowledge pertaining to Indonesia such as geography, history, or civics, let alone had much of a chance to immerse myself in the culture and lifestyle of the average Jakartan kid like I was supposed to be. As I grew older, I became cognizant of just how much my educational background had separated me from the locality of my country and my home culture. People in Indonesia sometimes come up to ask me where I'm from, only to find out I was just a locally raised kid who went to an international school with *BFE: big foreigner energy.*

MAKE YOURSELVES AT HOME

One time someone had asked me "Where are you a local at?" The thing is, even that gets confusing. How do you define locality, on the basis of legal registration? Where I spent the majority of my formative years? Where I align myself most with the local customs and values of that culture? I *feel* more like a local in Los Angeles because I fit and blend in with the society there a lot better, but I didn't grow up there. I think I *am* technically a local in Jakarta because I grew up there, but I don't fit and blend in with the society there. Don't get me wrong, I've always considered Jakarta my home for both emotional *and* legal reasons. It's just many times I asked myself how I was going to have the audacity to call myself a "local" in a country I barely even knew anything about.

I find it very confusing to explain where I'm from because I was born and raised for the first fifteen years of my life in Saudi Arabia, but I'm also American because I'm a citizen. I don't like answering that question based on the amount of time I lived in both countries. I want to say Saudi Arabia because I was born and raised there and most of my life has been there, but throughout my whole life I was told Saudi Arabia was just temporary and when my dad retired, we're going to live permanently in Los Angeles. However, I don't feel comfortable saying my home is Los Angeles because I've only lived here for one year and I don't feel like I've lived here long enough to say this is my home.

—SARAH KHOURI | SAUDI ARABIA & UNITED STATES

When I moved to LA, what I loved most about the city is it's welcoming of *all people* regardless of who they are and where they came from, which is why it's very quick and easy to feel right at home. Feeling at home in LA did come with complications, however. It was complicated whenever people back in college asked me whether I'd "go back home" for the holidays. For the majority of my four years, I was one of those international students who "going home" for, say Thanksgiving, meant heading back to my LA apartment, probably high as fuck after binging on homemade edibles (I love you California). I went to Seattle for a holiday with my friends, and a man had asked me where I was from, to which I responded LA. While that answer *was* the truth, it still felt like a lie. I wanted to add "I'm also from Jakarta," but decided against it to avoid rambling. Plus, he probably wouldn't have even known where it was.

To what extent do I get to also call LA my home? What's the criteria? Is there even one? Does living there on a four-year limited student visa, with no intentions of ever pursuing permanent residency or citizenship, constitute as a valid reason for declaring that place my second home? I struggled with the thought that perhaps it was inappropriate, or even audacious, of me to call LA home, especially around the people who actually grew up there their whole lives. Whenever claiming I'm a local doesn't satisfy the curiosity of the Indonesians asking me where I'm from every time I come back to Jakarta, I let them know I've *lived* in the States, or I was just *last from* there. It seems like an easy way out of having to go into too much depth explaining myself to them, but then they would say, "Oh, so you are from America," and I'm conflicted on how to respond. Do I get to say I'm from LA just because I've lived there? What's the limitation on the word "from" when it denotes where I was last physically located because I lived there, instead of denoting I was born and raised there?

Home has always been hard for me to define. I never connected with a country I lived in as much as I did with Indonesia. It's an incredibly special place with very special people. After high school, it's where all my friends were and where I went back to see family, but then my mom moved to Shanghai, so I never had the chance to go back. Now I often feel like there's no place I could really "return" to. There's a real loss I feel when other people discuss the concept of "home" and so clearly have an answer. I often feel like the longer I am away from Jakarta, the more my identity keeps slipping. The UK is nice, but London is often such an alienating place, there is really never a lot of comfort attached to being here. It makes me sad sometimes, the fact I don't have the funds to return to Indonesia anytime soon and there is a tiny part of me missing. I would, however, never claim I was from there as a white person. I had a strong connection with the country while living there and it will always be a part of my world, but I understand my limits of being able to "own" Indonesian culture which simply doesn't belong to me.

—REBECCA SANGS | CAMBODIA, GERMANY, UNITED

ARAB EMIRATES, INDONESIA, & CHINA

I think, more than just wanting to chase after a degree and career somewhere I was socially and linguistically somewhat more familiar with, what I wanted even more when I moved to Los Angeles was to find a place I could call home and feel like I wholeheartedly belonged. *Then I did.* When I moved there, I had the chance to meet people of every nationality, ethnicity, race, religion, background, passion, interest, and belief. I could stand in the intersection of all of these different groups and find little pieces of where I belonged in each of them. Similar to what I had at an international school but on a much larger scale of diversity—*like going from a fish tank to a whole ass ocean.*

Beyond the shallowness of power and prestige, on a deeper subconscious level I believe this is one of the truest reasons why the anglosphere remains such an attractive destination for internationals—especially for those like me who grew up more along the lines of cultural obscurity. One of the great things about the US, UK, Canada, and Australia—if not the greatest—is they are countries built by immigrants, for immigrants. They are melting pots where people from all walks of life and corners of the earth are able to come together, stay for as long or as short as they want, and be accepted for who they are. Despite what any politician or anyone else has to say, immigration and diversity have been, and always will be, at the core of what makes these nations special.

THE RHYTHM OF THE CITY

It's always interesting whenever I come home and meet with friends and family I haven't seen in a while. Whenever I meet up with childhood friends, or old high school peers and teachers, they always tell me how much I've changed. I, too, am often cognizant of how much living abroad has changed me as a person—as it should—but of course it's always so much more jarring to those who don't see the events that have taken place while I've been gone. Every time I return, I'm always a different version of myself than the last time I was here. At the same time, despite how long it's been and how far I've traveled, they also tell me I haven't changed all *that* much. Somehow, I'm still the same person I've always been. They're looking at a different hair color, a different body dressed in a different style, a different face listening to new beliefs and perspectives of the world, but they are still starring into the same pair of eyes and hearing the same voice. I think about how the way some people look at me and perceive those changes, must be the same way I look at Jakarta whenever I come back during the summer breaks, and it'll be same way I look at LA when I get to come back and visit in a few years from now.

Because, really, I'm not the only one who's changing. Home has changed as well and will continue to change. We often define home as *the place* with the people who make us feel like we most belong, where we were born, where our passports were issued, where we have citizenship rights, or where we own assets like a house or a business. For international and third-culture kids, all these things are neither absolutes nor constants. Passports and citizenship statuses are replaceable. Physical spaces erode; buildings and houses get demolished and rebuilt, and even countries and cities have fallen and emerged. Memories fade, or our perception of certain memories change over time. This street used to look different, that building used to not be there, there are all these new slang words I have never even heard of before, and all these new shops and restaurants have replaced some of the older ones I used to see in this part of town. Sometimes it's like I don't even recognize the city anymore, but other times the city is exactly how I always remembered it. Like a new rendition of an old song I grew up listening to, it's the same melody, just a different rhythm.

I often get asked where I feel more at home—Jakarta or Los Angeles? For years, I've lived between *here and there* and *there and here* so much, and now it's all blurred into one another. In truth, it's all become the same to me. I feel at home there, and I feel at home here. Some days I feel more at home there, and other days I feel more at home here. Heck, sometimes I don't even feel at home anywhere! We always leave so many pieces of ourselves behind in every place we've ever lived, sometimes I think it's hard to ever really feel *whole*. While it can be a very lonely and isolating experience, I think there is something so oddly fulfilling about it as well. How lucky are we that we get to call so many places home? When I think about it, it's not a lack of belonging, but an abundance of it. We don't just get to belong here, we get to also belong there, and we get to belong everywhere, and I think that's kind of beautiful.

On the one hand, growing up with a multicultural identity made me a permanent outsider. I'm always an "other." I can't speak to the experience of having gone to the same school, lived in the same place, and known the same people all my life. On the other hand, I think living abroad has made me much more open to new experiences and made me someone who is flexible and adaptable. Once I moved to the United States, I still got the question of "Where are you from?" I'd say, "I'm from here. I'm American," and they'd say, "but you weren't born here." Yes, but I was still born an American, and that part of my identity was just as valid regardless of where I grew up. In fact, I feel in many ways I am much more patriotic and more American having been brought up overseas because I could appreciate the freedoms Americans have, having lived in places where democracy—at the time when I was still a kid—was still only emerging in these parts of the world. It is that outsider's perspective that has allowed me to look at problems in slightly different ways, so I'm able to better serve now that I'm a US Senator.

—TAMMY DUCKWORTH

When people asked this question, I used to try and explain that I didn't really have a home. It seems like people who have lived in one place can't really understand this, so they usually keep pressing for a specific answer. Now I just say home is Nürnberg, which is the city closest to the small town my grandmother lives in. I have never actually spent any time living there, but it's the answer that satisfies people.

—LAURA HAETZEL | GERMANY, UNITED
STATES, SWITZERLAND, & AUSTRALIA

I was born in Hong Kong, but my family is from Singapore and Malaysia. I am not Thai, but I was raised in Thailand for most of my life and it is where I feel most at home and most familiar with a country. This can be hard to explain, especially when I am speaking to people who don't understand international students/third-culture kids/children of expatriates. It can also cause misunderstandings if I tell local Thai people that I am Thai, so usually the only time I will answer "Singaporean" is when Thai people ask me where I am from.

—CHARISSE TAN | SINGAPORE & THAILAND

My two "prepared" phrases are "I'm from South Korea, but my family's lived in Dubai for ten years," and "I'm South Korean, but I'm from Dubai." The first sounds unclear in a way, because it makes it sound like I don't associate with Dubai strongly, which is untrue. On the other hand, saying I'm "from" Dubai makes me worried sometimes, because people may take it as a flex or a way for me to dissociate from my ethnicity and identify with a wealthy, interesting, "elite" city, which is not what I'm trying to imply at all. It's all a balancing game, and sometimes I need to gauge the audience before choosing how to introduce myself. I'm not bitter about it or anything, I know this means I had a colorful, interesting upbringing with lots of stories to share, but it does take some thought.

—ESTHER EUNSUH PARK | SOUTH KOREA, SINGAPORE, & UNITED ARAB EMIRATES

Whenever people ask me where I am from, I usually say Indonesia. When I came to Canada for university, I realized sometimes it is hard for people to believe this, often prompting the question, "So where are you really from?" I neither look like the typical Indonesian, nor could I claim Indonesia to be part of my identity legally on any documents other than my birth certificate. I was born and raised in Indonesia, but my passport and nationality are Indian. As both countries play a role in my identity, I always have to clarify that although I am Indian, I was born and raised in Indonesia.

—DIVYA AGRAWAL | INDONESIA

I lived in India for nineteen years of my life since my birth, but I only began to experience the joy of life when I moved to LA, having met and becoming friends with like-minded people who were just as passionate, or even more, about film and everything else about life I found worthwhile. I may have physically grown during my first nineteen years in India, but it was only when I moved to LA that I had a personal, emotional, and professional growth in my life.

—MONISH PRAKASH | INDIA

No matter where I go in the world, I don't think locals accept me as "one of their own." When visiting Penang, I get asked where I'm from as if I'm a tourist, and people are surprised when I say I was born and raised there. Likewise, this happens in Singapore. I think my accent has a lot to do with it. Obviously, just by virtue of being Asian, I will never be fully accepted as a local Argentinian or Californian. There will always be the follow-up question, "but where are you really from?"

—LAURA JANE YEE | MALAYSIA,
ARGENTINA, & SINGAPORE

In my college, we usually ask "where do you consider home?" instead of "where are you from?" so it takes some pressure off from people to weigh their ethnicity against nationality against citizenship against racial identity when answering the question. When I tell people I consider Vietnam my home, they sometimes also get confused because I speak fluent Mandarin, but not Vietnamese. I used to feel very uncomfortable addressing the "where are you from?" question because I felt like I was "oversharing" or taking up too much of people's time when explaining the complexity of my upbringing, even though I know in my core both Vietnam and China are central to my identity.

—CARRIE SIYAN WANG | VIETNAM & CHINA

"Being raised" in a certain place defining my identity versus "where I come from" is very important to me, because I was adopted. Even though I am ethnically Vietnamese, and I wasn't born in France, I identify as being completely French, *because that is where I was raised my whole life, and that is where my family comes from.*

—ANH-LISE GILBERT | FRANCE

I think many people are surprised a Black person can have a multicultural and global upbringing, so when they meet me there's a whole lot of shock. In China and Thailand, the immediate assumption was I was from Africa, while in the US it's assumed I'm African American.

—TEN FRANCIS | UNITED STATES, THAILAND, & CHINA

Despite my citizenship and nationality being Austrian, I, even if only at heart, belong to the US just as much. So, I guess I'll go with the cheesy answer, but real nonetheless: Home is where my heart is.

—INA ZWIGL | AUSTRIA

ANGLOSPECTIVE

No one's bothering to learn or teach the history and culture of the places I'm from, so why do I need to bend my back to learn about countries that don't care about mine at all? It's things like this that still bother me, even five years later after graduating high school, because I know things haven't changed.

—TRISHA VARGAS | INDONESIA, HONG KONG, & PHILIPPINES

CHAPTER 4

THE INTERNATIONAL CHALLENGE TO WESTERN DOMINANCE

THE ANGLO LEAGUE

When I first came to the United States, many of my local friends and professors were shocked at how I knew so much about America despite never having been raised there. The real question should be how does one *not* know anything about a country the likes of America? Or even Canada, Australia, and the UK, though to a lesser degree than the US. Have you ever wondered why the world always seems to revolve around the anglosphere—the US and the UK in particular? Frankly, it's because it kind of does, and it sort of always has. There's an Anglospherist school of thought where one theory asserts the five core English-speaking nations (US, UK, Canada, Australia, and New Zealand) have not only managed to form their own distinctive branch within

Western history, but they are also becoming a distinctive leading civilization of their own.[11]

In other words, the anglosphere is a league of its own separated from the rest of the world as a group of super-power countries by virtue of their strong sociopolitical and economic influence, coupled with a robust military presence. CANZUK[12] has a combined GDP of more than six trillion dollars—right behind China and the entire European Union—and a combined population of 135 million people.[13] Now add that to the United States, which has the world's largest GDP of $21.4 trillion and a population of 328 million people.[14] All five countries, with the exception of New Zealand, are also some of the world's highest spenders when it comes to military defense.[15] All of this is to say in every sense of the word, as a group, they are absolutely *indomitable*.

DECOLONIZE INTERNATIONAL SCHOOLS

The assertion of Western hegemony was most evident to me through the colonization of international school curriculums. One of my required courses in the ninth grade was called Contemporary Issues in Asia, but I thought it was ironic how this was a school in Indonesia, an Asian country, and yet this class never even once touched upon Indonesian sociopolitical or economic affairs. In tenth grade, I

---

11 James Bennett, "The Emerging Anglosphere. (America and the West)," *ORBIS* Vol. 46, No. 1 (2001): 112.

12 CANZUK is the abbreviation used to reference Canada, Australia, New Zealand, and the United Kingdom as a collective.

13 Andrew Roberts, "It's Time to Revive the Anglosphere," *The Wall Street Journal*, August 8, 2020.

14 "United States," The World Bank, Accessed February 6, 2021.

15 "The 15 Countries with the Highest Military Spending Worldwide in 2019," Statista, Publication December 1, 2020.

had another mandatory course called Global Perspectives, but contrary to the course title, most of the class content only focused on Anglo-American narratives, and we learned about other countries and civilizations mainly through a Western-colonial perspective. I never really felt like I was receiving an international education so much as it felt like I was receiving a Western education, and we were only an international school by virtue of having a globally diverse student body. Mind you, up until this point, all of this was just the regular high school curriculum. I hadn't even started my *actual* international curriculum yet.

International schools promote an international education by adopting international curriculums such as the International Baccalaureate, Advanced Placement, NAPLAN, and Cambridge to foster global mindedness. I was enrolled in both the International Baccalaureate and Advanced Placement in high school from the eleventh grade throughout twelfth. I took IB Music, and most of our musical education was largely centered around European and American pieces and composers, while rarely touching upon works from other cultures like Asia, Africa, and Latin America—all simply categorized under the umbrella of "world music." I took AP Macroeconomics, and not once did they ever focus on economic development outside of the Western Hemisphere.

While I want to say the IB Indonesian course, during the time of my enrollment, did the best it could to improve my language proficiency—especially for it being a standard *second-language* program—I still found after two years of being in that course (and two more additional years of Indonesian language classes prior to that), I had graduated knowing almost nothing about Indonesian geography, history, or civics. I knew a lot about the founding fathers of the United

States and World Wars I and II, but not once was I ever taught about one of the greatest and most powerful empires in the history of Indonesia and all of Southeast Asia, *Majapahit*. I knew there was an American Pledge of Allegiance, but not an Indonesian Youth Pledge (*Sumpah Pemuda*). I knew the names of almost all fifty states of America and the four countries of the United Kingdom, but not the major islands of Indonesia and how many there even were.

Looking back now, *respectfully,* I laugh at the thought. Twelve years of a supposedly "globally inclusive" education, and I had completed my primary and secondary education knowing everything about the US, UK, and Western-world affairs and nothing about my own country or the rest of the non-Western world. Keep in mind the ludicrousness of all this lies in the fact that the Independent School Councils research data indicates as of January 2021, there are now over twelve thousand international K–12 schools worldwide educating over six million students, and approximately 80 percent of enrollments are mainly children of local families attending these institutions in their native country.[16] Majority of these enrollments are concentrated in the UAE, China, Saudi Arabia, and India.[17]

Many international schools—whether it's through the implementation of a curriculum, adoption of textbooks and other forms of classroom paraphernalia, or administering language rules on campus—enforce a form of Anglo-American propaganda in that they present idealized forms of the West, thereby implicitly colonizing the minds of young

---

16 "About the International Schools Market," ISC Research, Accessed February 6, 2021

17 "Annual survey finds continued growth in international schools," *ICEF Monitor,* Publication September 5, 2018.

learners by making us more amenable to Western concerns. When I think about it, it's definitely one of the reasons why many of us international students end up pursuing our higher education and/or careers there. Our education has prepped and primed us to thrive and excel there and conditioned us to think it is the only sensible option. My international schooling made me aware of how the political could affect the pedagogical.

ISOLATED

The anglosphere is very detached from the rest of the world, and not just from a power standpoint. Except for the United Kingdom, which is surrounded by a cluster of other European nations, Australia, New Zealand, Canada, and the United States are geographically very isolated from other countries. Whenever I told people in the US I was from Indonesia, the most common reaction was always "Where's that?" On the one hand, I feel like this is just one of those experiences that comes with being from an "unpopular country." Nobody would really know anything about us or where we are unless they had a particular reason to. Though, in my experience, even some of the most *woke* Americans I know are sometimes (no offense) not the most geographically competent people.

Obviously, there could be a long list of possible reasons to explain this. Physical distance could also be one of those reasons, where they're so secluded amongst themselves that they've never really bothered knowing where everyone else was. It's been a rather disappointing experience when every time I mention Indonesia, it is often met with questions or comments that, while I understand come with innocuous intentions, are also just *bewilderingly ignorant*. I've heard everything from "What country is Indonesia in?" to "Is Jakarta a part of China?" A student I once roomed with for a school trip asked me if Indonesia was "near Korea," where she was going to spend the next semester studying abroad, and when I told her we're "more south of Asia," she asked if that meant we were "next to Africa."

Sometimes people often get confused when I tell them I am Asian, not realizing India is also in Asia.

—UTKARSH MEHTA | INDIA

A lot of people always assume I speak Spanish just because I'm from South America. I'm from Brazil. We speak Portuguese.

—ANNA BEATRIZ FERRONATO PIMENTEL | BRAZIL

I've often wondered if it is this physical isolation that has contributed to more than just bad geography skills. When you think about it, the anglosphere is not just physically isolated from the rest of the world, they're culturally isolated as well. It's no secret the people there tend to just live in their own little *first-world, Western* bubble and generally have a weak understanding of what the real world outside of the sphere is like. Jakarta is the largest city in Southeast Asia and one of the most populated *urban* agglomerations on Earth.[18] I always have to tell people that otherwise they run along with the image of me living in bungalows or huts in the middle of a rice paddy field, chilling next to Sumatran tigers.

---

18   "Jakarta Population 2021," World Population Review, Accessed February 6, 2021.

Or they think of me jumping off waterfalls in the middle of luscious evergreen jungles, like that's the kind of everyday shit I would do. Some people are still surprised by the fact we have things like Wi-Fi, electric cars, and get shocked when I show them pictures of the central business district where there are lots of tall office buildings, luxurious five-star hotels, high-end shopping malls, and skyscrapers.

There was a boy in one of my freshman seminars who asked if I knew what Netflix was, and another student asked if we "wore normal clothes in Indonesia" after I told her we're a Muslim-majority country. People have asked me if we carried brands like Apple, ZARA, Gucci, or Ferraris, and they have asked if we have wild animals like monkeys or boars roaming around the streets. I had an Indonesian friend come over to my dorm to chill with me, and that same Vietnamese American roommate I mentioned earlier, just so casually asked us, "So, do you guys still have slaves in Indonesia?" Whether it was Americans or foreigners from other countries I ran into, a lot of the times when they asked me what my life in Indonesia was like, they always expected to hear crazy answers to fulfill stereotypical exotic fantasies of foreign cultures abroad.

When I told my friend I came from Saudi Arabia, she was so confused, but happy at the same time because she knows there are camels there. She then thought, for a whole day, I had a pet camel! When I found out, I could not stop laughing. I later told her I didn't have a pet camel, and to this day we still laugh about it.

—**SARAH KHOURI** | **SAUDI ARABIA & UNITED STATES**

In truth, the most difficult thing I had to deal with throughout my time living in America was not only having people constantly making assumptions of the place where I was from, but also making assumptions about my intelligence, my character, my personality, and my competence solely based off of it. One day I was chilling in my dorm room having a conversation with my Vietnamese American roommate. Somewhere in the middle of our conversation, we were both laughing, and she goes, "Yeah, oh my God, and by the way, my parents thought you were poor!" I was so taken aback by the bluntness of that comment, and then she explained. When she told her parents I was from Jakarta, they didn't know it was the capital city. They thought Bali was the capital, and Jakarta was just some other random Indonesian city. Based off this, they told her she needed to be careful because they made the assumption I was poor and would therefore steal her belongings.

Remember that business fraternity I talked about earlier? That same friend in the fraternity who told us they rejected Jenna because they said her English wasn't good enough also told us they rejected me because "Indonesians aren't smart enough." Indeed, out of all of the international students hailing from countries like Vietnam, Indonesia, Myanmar, and India who rushed for this fraternity that year, the only one who got accepted hailed from Hong Kong. I had applied to two different English tutoring jobs on campus. After telling them I was an international student from Indonesia, both interviewers felt the need to probe me (to what I thought were very excessive lengths) on whether my English would be good enough to—and I am quoting one of the interviewers—"be helping native English speakers with their essays."

During my Women and Genders Studies class freshman year, I was in front of the board taking down notes of key words the professor wanted me to write down from our class discussion. For context, I was the only international student in that class. One of the words that came up was a term that had the word "fuck" in it, and then out of nowhere the professor paused the discussion and requested someone else from the class to come up to the front and write down the word *for me* instead. I stood there and looked at her with a confused expression on my face, and she directed her response to the entire class, like I'm some sort of case study, and said "Some people from different cultures are not comfortable swearing, especially in a different language." How ironic this was a class focused on empowering women of color and defying stereotypes, and yet here she was actively subscribing to the notion that just because I'm a woman from an Asian country I would be so docile and timid as to not ever do anything as bold as to *swear in a foreign language.*

Junior year, I took an entrepreneurship class taught by an adjunct professor. For context, there were only three international students including myself, and I was the only female. One day I raised my hand to answer a question, and I didn't even so much as stutter or utter a single word before the professor cut me off and asked, "Can I ask, what's your first language?" I saw other students raising their eyebrows and squinting their eyes around the room in my peripheral, and I replied back "English." He asked again, "No, I mean, what's your primary language?" I replied again, "English." He then asked again, for the third time, "What is the language you are most comfortable speaking in?" I replied again, for the third time, "English." He looked at me, shrugged, and said, "Go on, then." What am I even supposed to make of that incident?

THE COLONIZATION OF MEDIA AND INFORMATION

It's disheartening—to say the least—to realize *this* is the manner in which people from other societies view you, your people, and your country. To be honest, can I blame them? Should we even be surprised when we know that's *all* they ever see about us in media? We often only hear about the same group of countries, most of whom—if not all—are only in the spotlight out of their relation to the US or UK, though albeit I believe this has started changing in more recent years with the rise of countries like China and South Korea. Blame it on the media always portraying the rest of the world as these undeveloped civilizations riddled with humanitarian crises and diseases, or exoticized versions of stereotypical fantasies come to life.

Sometimes I get comments like, "Oh, you're from Germany? Where the Nazis are?" Or the "Oh, Hitler's Germany," which just shows you how uneducated some of these people really are.

—VALEA METZGER | GERMANY

They ask me about Pablo Escobar, or Sofia Vergara; they think all the women are super curvy and dance like Shakira. They've asked me what cocaine tastes like. I've never even seen cocaine in my entire life.

—SOFIA PEDRAZA-BOLIVAR | COLOMBIA & CANADA

Arabs and Middle Eastern people are always portrayed as terrorists who like to blow up mosques and white people, and all the women there are oppressed and forced to be covered from head to toe with only the eyes showing.

—ZAINAH AL ESSA | KUWAIT

They always assumed I was escaping some horrible condition like poverty. They even asked about how I found my school from "all the way in Africa," not understanding the fact the internet is also a thing there.

—SHALOM WANYONI | KENYA

You see, lack of geographical vicinity is no longer the insuperable barrier it once was prior to living in the age of the worldwide web. Along with other advances to transportation and communication, digital media has allowed people from all over the world to acquire information and knowledge about one another from within the comforts of their own homes. However, while access to the internet is quickly being democratized on a global scale, there is still a large gap in our ability to have an authentic understanding of other cultures. Often times, the only resources available to most people to learn about the outside world is through online media, which is heavily dictated by the Western world, particularly America.

The US represents a third of the global media and entertainment (M&E) industry, making it the largest in the world.[19] Their prominence in the global flow of cultural

---

19　"The Media and Entertainment Industry in the United States," Select USA, Accessed February 6, 2021.

products—everything from motion pictures, television programs and commercials, streaming content, music and audio recordings, broadcast, radio, book publishing, and video games—and economic activity has placed them at the center of all international attention and interaction. There have been studies on the role of the media in international relations that observed how media flowing from the US to the rest of the world constituted a soft power that has made the US a global hegemonic force starting in the 1990s.[20] A study on globalization of culture through media examines the cultural imperialism theory and argues audiences worldwide are affected heavily by media emanating particularly from Western industrialized nations like the US and the UK.[21]

These countries have not only practically colonized international media, but they've also colonized international information. Research by the GEONET project at the Oxford Internet Institute shows the internet generally remains heavily skewed toward rich, Western countries.[22] If you are using Google to search for local information in Canada or Australia, you will be directed to primarily locally produced content about them, but if you're in Sierra Leone, Pakistan, or Indonesia, despite their large population sizes, there is relatively little content about them in Google search results.[23] What

20 Filiz Coban, "The Role of the Media in International Relations: From the CNN Effect to the Al-Jazeere Effect," *Journal of International Relations and Foreign Policy* Vol. 4, No. 2 (2016): 49.

21 Marwan M. Kraidy, "Globalization of culture through the media. In J. R. Schement (Ed.)," *Encyclopedia of Communication and Information* Vol. 2 (2002): 360.

22 "Digital Hegemonies: The Localness of Search Engine Results," Geonet at the Oxford Internet Institute, Published May 4, 2017.

23 Mark Graham and Anasuya Sengupta, "We're All Connected Now, So Why Is the Internet So White and Western?" *The Guardian*, Published October 5, 2017.

little information there is, the content is produced by out-siders—particularly, those from the West.

A study on digital hegemonies conducted by the same aforementioned institution reveals the United States alone supplies over half of the first-page content on Google.[24] This means US-produced content is not only highly visible in much of the rest of the world, but also highly consumed by the rest of the world. It is this visibility that has enabled America and the West to infiltrate the international space so much it has become the lens through which people from other countries are able to view the world, and that's danger-ous. When all our knowledge and understanding of the world has been presented to us solely through an Americanized and westernized point of view, it fails to deliver accurate representation and exposure of the rest of the world. This creates real consequences and further amplifies geograph-ical and cultural biases in a world already heavily riven by stereotypes and discrimination.

I had this one colleague at one of the companies I used to work for who straight up told me he was a Trump supporter and US army veteran, and therefore disliked people from China. Funny enough, the company I worked for was a Japanese car manufacturing company, and all the parts used there were imported from China.

—DIAO HONG SU | CHINA

24 "Digital Hegemonies: The Localness of Search Engine Results," Geonet at the Oxford Internet Institute, Published May 4, 2017.

CHALLENGING THE NARRATIVE

By extension of the West's influence on our ability to see the world, it has also influenced how we are able to see ourselves. Proximity to whiteness—whether it be through speaking a white language, having a whiter skin color, being immersed in white culture, marrying into a white family, or having Caucasian blood run through you and/or your children's veins—is not just something merely admired and praised by people in the non-Western world. People often pay a ridiculous premium to be able to come close, and they centralize their sense of self-worth around it.

Indonesia is one of those countries with something I've labeled as *low-self-esteem culture*. The other country that comes to mind is the Philippines because I once saw this meme of two arms—one arm on one side representing Indonesians and the other Filipinos—coming together in an epic handshake and in the middle it said, "Hating our national identities." In case you were wondering, I was born in 1997, and kids like me who grew up outside of the anglosphere were brought up during a time of massive Anglo-Western dominance. History has always painted the colonizers (the West) as virtuous heroes and the colonized as impoverished damsels in distress waiting for their white knight in shining armor. We were made to know everything about the Western world, about the Americans and the British and how influential they are, about the Canadians and the Australians and how powerful they also are by proxy of their relationships with the US and the UK. We know where in the world these countries are, and we hear pretty much everything that goes on with them on the news (albeit mostly the US and UK)—everything from politics to pop culture. For the rest of the world, we never just merely admired them from afar, we aspired to be like them so much some of us ended up hating ourselves.

There's a common phrase in Indonesia called "kacang lupa kulit." It translates to "peanut forgets its skin," which talks about one forgetting where their roots are from. Most Indonesians are pretty patriotic in my opinion. Most would judge other Indonesians for not being "Indonesian enough." The same is true vice versa. I reckon there are also a lot of Indonesians who want to stray as far as they can from their Indonesian roots.

—RAFAEL RAFKA-SULISTIO BUNAWAN | INDONESIA

The truth is I have had to teach myself how to be proud and comfortable in my Indonesian skin. Most Indonesians, especially those of my generation and below, are just not. We see it in not only how we tend to admire other cultures more than our own, and envy foreigners from more well-known or more developed countries, we also see it in how we regard ourselves in comparison to them. It's almost fashionable to put our own people down and say people from other countries are smarter than us, cooler than us, and more attractive than us because they're fairer in color or have more Eurocentric features than us. We address them with higher regard than we do our own people, and we prefer the idea of befriending them, being seen hanging out with them, or taking pictures with them because we think it boosts our social status. We almost never see Indonesia acknowledged on the global stage, at least not for anything that actually depicts us in an appealing or desirable manner.

And when you've never seen yourself in books or movies or music, the first time you do—or that rare occurrence you do—can be absolutely life-changing. Because if we've never been given the space to see that we can become hugely successful figures—international best-selling authors from Indonesia, world-renowned doctors from Bangladesh, scientists from Guatemala, successful corporate leaders from Kenya, entrepreneurs from Qatar, world-famous athletes from Iran, and the next big international superstars from Thailand—then we never will be.

As someone who went to an international school, it makes me sad to even call it that. What we are taught is all US and European-centric. I barely knew anything about Kenyan history. I learned a bit about Kenyan culture in elementary school, but overall, we were hardly educated about the past and present issues faced by the country we reside in. I think it's a problem all international schools face. The racist history of international schools and how they were created for the children of white missionaries or diplomats and expatriates is still perpetuated today with the lack of academic diversity and pedagogy, as well as by the people who are admitted to these schools. It deepens class division and is seen as an elite institution in which some people pay more money for their K–12 education than they will for university.

—ANONYMOUS | NEPAL & KENYA

If Africa is ever brought up, generally it's mostly talked about in the context of poverty or slavery. I try to incorporate more of African cultures or Nigerian culture as much as possible into my education (e.g., my IB extended essay or my IB art exhibitions) to present a more authentic perspective of Africa. It's been tough because as a British Nigerian born and raised in the UK, I feel extremely disconnected from my African roots, but I try my best to educate myself about it outside of school.

—MICHAELA JOHNSON | UNITED KINGDOM

Going to an international school made me very distant from the culture of my country of origin (Taiwan). When I moved to Indonesia, I thought I could find a new place to feel a sense of belonging, but instead I ended up blending into the group of *other international students who were just as confused about their identities as I was because we were all just too westernized. Throughout my primary and secondary education, I've barely learned anything about Taiwan or Indonesia. I've always felt lost and ashamed for not knowing the cultures of these two places when I get asked about them.*

—ARIELLE JUAN | TAIWAN & INDONESIA

We learned a lot about American history, and we had a lot of options to learn about American topics, but rarely did we have a choice to learn about Hong Kong or Asian history. I've learned more about Asian history in America than I did in my high school back in Hong Kong. I had to learn about Asian history on my own time.

— ANONYMOUS | HONG KONG

One of the feedback comments I received from my teacher for my IB global politics assessment presentation was to choose a topic related to the US to keep my work relevant for the IB examiners. I felt like a lot of the concepts were mostly either Afrocentric or Americentric. The class talked a lot about politics in the US, but I remember my friends and I wanting to discuss the Indonesian presidential debate that was happening at that time instead.

—MATTHEW ONG | INDONESIA

Because my father's first language isn't English, and my mother came from a mixed cultural upbringing, it meant sometimes words and feelings were misunderstood. But as soon as we all sat together at the dinner table, any hurt feelings were washed away by the comfort and understanding brought through our meals.

—SOPHIE BURKHARDT | HONG KONG

CHAPTER 5

ALL AROUND THE WORLD IN A FEW DISHES

THE TASTE OF HOME

You don't need me to say much about how food is an important part of our lives. The significance of food goes beyond satiating us on a physical level, providing essential nutrients to supplement our biological development, and affecting our psychophysiology. There is an intangible emotional quality of food that can never be fully and accurately encapsulated by food writers, scientists, chefs, travel documentarians, *let alone me.* It's intrinsic to human nature to form a personal bond with our food, but when you come from a multinational background, or have perhaps adopted a multicultural identity, there is a whole other level of intimacy that gets created in our relationship with our meals. More than just an extension of our culture, it is also oftentimes our coping mechanism for homesickness, and it is how we connect with other people. It's more than just missing the authentic taste of the cuisine we've left behind. We miss the human element and sentimental values attached to food as well.

The way I grew up with food at home is very mixed and diverse. I come from a Chinese Indonesian household, so naturally I would eat dishes like *Ku Chai Kwe, Tau Swan,* and *Kwe Cap* on the Chinese side, and *Empal Empuk, Rendang Sapi,* and *Ayam Gulai* on the Indonesian side. Being raised by a single mom meant we would always have to eat out or order takeout because she never had the time to cook at home. Some of my fondest childhood memories of eating with my mom are filled with images of *Paneer Makhani* with *Naan* or *Chicken Biryani,* a steaming bowl of sticky white rice with *Natto* served on the side, feasting on some *yangnyeom galbi,* and slurping up a bowl of *naengmyeon.* My primary school days remind me of eating *pinoy* spaghetti cooked by my Filipino teachers and drinking a cold box of *Teh Botol* after school from the *warung* right across campus. I could smell the sweet scent of *sate ayam* cooking on the charcoal grill, the savory and spicy flavors of *mie goreng Jawa* freshly cooked on the side of the street. When I think of childhood treats, I think of *kaju katli* I'd get from our Indian neighbor next door, boxes of *Unagi Pie* my mother's Japanese clients would bring back for us, and a cold glass of *achim haetsal* from the local Korean supermarket as my midday snack.

Home tastes like the smell of basil and oregano and the taste of fresh burrata, good prosciutto, red wine, warm spicy Salteñas with a nice cold Paceña beer for lunch one day, and the next a chilled focaccia at night, with Spritz and mozzarella in carrozza for aperitivo.

—RAQUEL CHAVEZ CORS | BOLIVIA, ITALY, VENEZUELA, & CHILE

To me, home is more of a smell than a taste. Our foods are usually cooked with a lot of different smelling spices, and they are cooked over long periods of time. Every time I would walk into our house, the smell of food is what would me hit me first. I could smell so many different street foods just walking down the street, and I think that's I what I miss more than even the taste of the actual food.

—SHALOM WANYONI | KENYA

Home is a taste that is hard to encapsulate into words. It's not only something that is hard to bring back with us from home, but also something that is hard to find abroad whenever we find ourselves missing it the most. There is a general public consensus that food in the anglosphere is typically "bland," or less flavorful compared to a lot of other parts of the world. We often even see this satirized on social media, *the fact white people colonized half of the world for spices and yet they still don't know how to season their food beyond salt and pepper.* While this is anecdotally apparent, it has even been proved to be scientifically apparent on a molecular level as well. I came across a study on flavor network and the principles of food pairing that examines the general patterns which determine what ingredients are combined when creating dishes in different parts of the world. Boiling down all the scientific jargon in there to make it more *digestible* for your *consumptive pleasures* (puns intended), for all intents and purposes of this chapter, this is the part I want us to focus on:

Simply put, there are two "elements" that create a dish—the ingredients, and the number of shared compounds existing between them. The number of shared compounds dictate the flavors—the greater that number, the more alike they are in their molecular gastronomy, hence the lesser the flavor, and vice versa. What the study found was that Asian and Southern European cuisines have the tendency to avoid combining ingredients that *don't* share flavor compounds (different ingredients), and it is that contrast which attributes to a richness in flavor. By contrast, North American and Western European cuisines have a higher inclination toward creating recipes using ingredients that *do* share flavor compounds (like-ingredients).[25] This is why, to people from other parts of the world that do not share the same culinary practices as North Americans and Western Europeans, the food there tends to be perceived by their tongues to be less flavorful, relative to what they are used to. Cooking is just as much a science as it is an art, so the next time you sit there staring at a bowl of overly-mayonnaised potato salad and a plate of unseasoned chicken breasts thinking *what on God's green earth is this shit*, just know your disdain is perfectly valid.

FOOD DIARY

As college students, not only are we typically on a tighter budget or enrolled in student meal plans, we're also constantly running on very tight schedules. Eating just becomes a matter of what is the least expensive and least time-consuming option that is going to sustain us for the greatest amount of time. Frankly, this is universal among all college students. As international students, however, not only do we have to adjust to this aspect of change in our eating habits, but we

---

25   Yong Yeol Ahn, Sebastian E. Ahnert, James P. Bagrow and Albert-László Barabási, "Flavor Network and The Principles of Food Pairing," *Scientific Report* Vol.1, No.196 (2011): 3-4.

also have to get accustomed to either not eating certain foods or eating more of other foods than what we've been used to our whole lives. I went from eating rice for one or two meals a day everyday all my life, to maybe only once a month if not even less once I moved to America. The transition to eating more bread or potato-based meals felt a little weird for me at first because back home, bread is more often considered a snack, or an ingredient incorporated into a dessert or breakfast. Potatoes are also usually eaten with rice, which I definitely would have gotten mortified stares for in a state like California where consuming carbs is basically the equivalent of selling your soul to the devil.

My first year of college, I was so turned off by the food in the US I lost 8 kg. Basically, "freshman fifteen" happened in the opposite way for me because I preferred eating less than having to put myself through bad food.

—ANH-LISE GILBERT | FRANCE

My general and personal experience of eating in America has basically been boiled down to: If it's relatively cheap and tasty, it's most likely very unhealthy. If it's healthy and made with high quality ingredients, it may or may not be all that tasty, but it's definitely going to be very expensive. The typical *healthy* American meal consists largely of an endless plethora of sandwiches, wraps, and salads, which I could only take so much of before I'd *fucking lose it* if I had to take another bite out of a bowl of quinoa salad with half an organic avocado and a bottle of overpriced kombucha. However, the typical diet of most Americans, I've noticed, consists mostly of burgers with fries, fried chicken, hotdogs, pizzas, and the usual diabetes-inducing foods you'd *stereotypically* associate with American cuisine. They're delicious, but there's only so many levels and combinations of deep-fried bread and meat slathered in ketchup, mustard, or mayo before they all just start tasting the same to me.

The other part of that is if it's healthy, made with high quality ingredients, and expensive, the portion sizes in America are *normal.* If it's cheaper, tastier, and a lot unhealthier, the portion sizes are *absolutely fucking humongous.* The thing about food in Indonesia is yes, we do eat a lot of meats, fruits, and vegetables, but we eat a lot more carbs. *Hell, we eat carbs on top of carbs.* We have a lot of rich, flavorful sauces that are very thick and fatty. A lot of Indonesian food is deep fried in what's most likely refined oil, and we can't live without our desserts usually loaded with palm sugar and coconut milk. We can make fun of Americans all we want, but both cuisines are actually very unhealthy. The difference is just that Americans eat bigger quantities than we do. It's no secret serving portions in the US are *beyond astronomical.* Adjusting to the enormous food sizes in America—from meals, drinks, to even snacks like candy bars and chips—was so difficult for someone who's only 4'11, 105 pounds, and lived alone. I drank out of soda cups taller than the size of my head and let's just say, I am never ordering a large-sized popcorn from the movie theaters ever again.

But perhaps the most *mind-blowing* thing when I first came to the US was seeing just how many options there are for *everything.* Don't get me wrong; we have a lot of food options back in Indonesia, too, but nowhere near as large and as assorted as in America. One food item can come in over a dozen or a hundred different variations according to source, size, ingredient components, packaging, and combinations of flavors I never even knew could exist together. On the one hand, it was a little overwhelming at times whenever I'd go to Target knowing all I wanted was to just *go get milk,* and I'm standing there in front of twenty different varieties of milk—non-fat milk, 3.25 percent fat milk, skimmed, oat, soy, almond, cashew, coconut, rice, hemp, macadamia, even flax seed and quinoa milk—not knowing which one I should choose.

On the other hand, there are so many alternatives to everything that it makes having special dietary requirements so much easier. When I finally hit the point in my life where I started exercising regularly and stopped having the diet of a teenage stoner, it was so easy for me to find healthy alternatives like chickpea pastas, plant-based meats, and tasty and healthy snacks to help me lose all that extra weight. It's actually quite ironic that for how bad of a reputation America has for being unhealthy, in my opinion it's actually so much easier to eat healthy there—*if you have the money for it and are not living with your parents anymore.* Every summer I come back to Jakarta, my mother feeds me like I'm training for a food-eating competition, so I come back to LA looking like an overstuffed pet chinchilla. Whenever I leave Indonesia, I find I always miss flavors, but whenever I leave LA, I always miss specific foods I can't find anywhere else—like the raspberry cashew milk overnight oats I always grabbed to eat on the way to school or work. I miss Whole Food's lemon cranberry quinoa, and certain restaurants or food vendors like Tsujita, my neighborhood farmer's market, and Pepe's Tacos.

Not only that, but I could eat healthier and in a shorter amount of kitchen prep time. Many of my meals did not really involve me cooking, but more so it was just me putting together a bunch of packaged ingredients into an edible and somewhat more appetizing meal. Simplistic seasoning requirements make American and Western European cuisines relatively easier and faster to whip up, like Americanized pastas or salads with only three ingredients. Indonesian and Chinese cooking takes over an hour to prep and cook the ingredients, and five minutes to devour the whole fucking thing. God bless America and their tendency to pre-package everything, and I mean *everything*. A lot of ingredients like garlic, onions, bell-peppers, and corn have already been cut and prepped for you. *They even have microwavable soup in a jar, and egg whites in a carton.* It's a luxury I had forgotten did not exist back in Indonesia. When I went to my local grocery store and asked the salesman where the pre-chopped potatoes were, he thought I was referring to frozen fries.

AT THE TABLE

Western culture is very individualistic, whereas many other cultures are more collectivistic. This is really one of the key themes throughout this book we'll keep revisiting in later chapters, but in this one we see how this even affects the way people from different cultures sit down and eat. Whenever I would go out with my American peers, they're more likely to order their own dish and offer me a bite or two of their foods in exchange for mine, whereas my international peers and I would always order family style where we order a bunch of different dishes and share them in the middle. This difference in culture also affects the way we split the bill, which was perhaps the biggest thing I had to get used to when it came to eating with certain friends. When I went out to grab lunch with an American friend, it was already established we would order our own dishes and pay separate bills. Come the time to pay, they had asked me to split. I was confused as to why the sudden change of plans, before realizing perhaps it was because I had asked them for a bit of their food in exchange for some of mine earlier on during the meal (at least, to my understanding). Coming from my culture, it was hard to not initially see this as stingy behavior, but I've had to train myself over the years to learn to view it from a different cultural perspective. I don't think the intention is to be stingy, but to be fair and to treat everybody as an equal.

When I invited an American friend to one of my birthday lunches, they responded saying they would love to go, but they were a little short on cash and didn't have the money to spend. At first, I thought they were perhaps talking about money for transportation, and then it hit me they thought they were going to have to pay on *my* birthday, which caught me by surprise that they had even thought that. In my culture, we treat our friends on our birthdays as a token of our appreciation for their friendship and presence at the event. On the other hand, on another occasion, I got invited to an American friend's birthday dinner, and I was shocked when they brought out the bill and everyone, except for the birthday boy, started throwing in their credit cards to pay. I then learned in Western culture friends will split the bill equally as a way to treat them on their birthdays. It was then quite funny when I had gotten invited to a first-generation African American friend's birthday dinner. They were raised in the US, but their parents were African, so toward the end of the dinner I was just waiting to see whether the African side was going to prevail and take on the entire bill, or the American side was going to make me whip out my card.

We typically don't enforce the Dutch pay system too extremely. I'll pay for you this time, you'll pay next time. It's an unspoken rule that doesn't seem to be understood by friends from less similar cultures. When I pay for them once, they don't feel the need to reciprocate the favor. If I pay this time, they'll still make me split the bill next time.

—THENNY WIDJAJA | INDONESIA

I've noticed there is a different standard of acceptance when it comes to not only which animal to eat, but which parts of an animal to eat. I've learned animal consumption in the West tends to avoid using the entire carcass of the animal. My mother is one of those hardcore Asian ladies who will cook an entire dead chicken into a pot. No joke, you will see everything from the feet, the whole head with eyes, nostrils, and tongue still inside its beak, *and even the genitals.* Maybe to people in the anglosphere it's viewed as a little extreme, but I think in most other cultures it's actually normal to see the head of the fish or eat organs like the skin and tails. I remember eating take-home *Jī jiǎo* in the dorm while I had some white group members come over, and it didn't occur to me most Westerners would freak out over seeing a pair of braised *chicken feet* on the plate. They just sat there, in my dorm, and stared at me eating chicken feet while making disgusted facial expressions. It was not the best way to enjoy my dish within the comforts of my own living space.

I try to avoid things that seem "exotic" to Canadian students, so basically anything other than North American foods. I only eat Afghani food with my family around or by myself. I try to avoid having anyone see what I eat as my floormates in university said I only enjoy food from low GDP countries, and it made me very self-conscious about what I was eating.

—KATHERINE BOUDREAU | ITALY, UNITED
KINGDOM, BELGIUM, GERMANY, UNITED
ARAB EMIRATES, & CANADA

There is even a different standard as to how certain foods should be eaten in the West. It's almost considered audacious to eat pizza or hot dogs with silverware. Burgers, fries, and chicken wings should be eaten with the hands, but not rice, fish, or other meats and vegetables. I find it interesting considering rice originates in China, and nine out of the top ten producers of rice by country are all in the Asian hemisphere, where people customarily eat rice with either their hands or Chopsticks anyway.[26] Keep in mind it was through widespread British and European colonization that made the practice of eating with a fork the epitome of proper dining etiquette around the world.[27] Technically, this means many people in the West reap the pleasures of Asian cuisine without bother learning the authentic way of eating it. It's considered inappropriate to eat rice with our hands and is viewed as strange if not boorish and uncultured, *but somehow it's considered cultured to eat rice with a fork.*

I remember a time when this girl I shared a class with talked about how she went to a "medieval style" restaurant where they

---

26   "Leading countries based on the production of milled rice in 2018/2019 (in million metric tons)," *Statista,* Publication February 2020.

27   "Facts and History of Eating Utensils," *Eating Utensils,* Accessed on February 26, 2016.

"eat with their hands and all that gnarly shit." Microaggressions like that make me hesitant to eat with my hands in public.

—SOPHIE RONODIPURO | INDONESIA

TASTE THE NATIONS

Of course, it is to be expected there are going to be people we meet in college who are not so open to trying new foods. For the record, anybody from any culture is susceptible to this close-mindedness, but in my experience, it's never been the international students. Unfortunately, I've had experiences with some of my American friends where I felt like they were being disrespectful toward my cultural dishes. I remember a friend of mine coming over to my apartment and I offered them crepe cake my friend's mom packed for me to bring back. When I told them it was Durian, they were immediately repulsed and said, "I'd rather die than eat that smelly shit." I asked them if they've ever even had Durian before, and they said "No, but I know it smells nasty." No smell came out of the cake. It's one thing to say you don't like a certain food because you know it from experience, but to close-mindedly hop on a bandwagon of naysayers without considering the insensitivity of your words is another.

I remember one occasion where I saw a person at a party eating a Pork Floss snack from home, which I was really happy to see and asked to share. However, another one of my friends thought that particular snack was disgusting, which I felt was uncalled for as he had never tried the snack and was basing this purely on the idea of what the snack was.

— GEORGE HENRY RICHARD JOLLY | HONG KONG

However, that is only one bad experience out of many wonderful experiences I've had in being able to share my cuisines with friends of other cultures. In truth, I had the idea of writing a chapter dedicated to food because I remembered, back in high school, one of our biggest annual school events I always looked forward to the most every year was United Nations (UN) Day. Everyone would come to school dressed in their traditional garments, and parents would cook food from their respective cultures. Different areas of campus would be dedicated to a certain region of the world, where we could visit each of them and indulge in food from the different countries. I almost felt like whatever petty high school *beef* (pun intended, again) any of us had with one another sort of went away for just that one day because everyone was just too busy stuffing their faces (that, and most of our parents were there).

It was really what showed me how sharing cuisine is one of the easiest and quickest ways, and the most intimate way, for people to not only share our cultures, but also bridge our differences. When I look back at my college days, some of my most beautiful and cherished memories are the ones shared at the dining table: taking my Mexican friends to the Indonesian restaurant in LA for the first time and debating which culture has the spiciest foods, inviting a white friend to come eat Korean BBQ with my mom and I, eating dim-sum with my Black friend in Chinatown, eating *soondubu jjigae* after a night of getting blitzed at a party with my friends at three in the morning, and I can only hope I will get to create more of these memories in the future.

I never cooked home food in my house in the US because I lived with roommates who were very unfamiliar with South Asian food. However, one day my aunt taught me one of my mom's recipes, and I knew I had to recreate it. Once I had sautéed the onions and garlic, everyone came out of their rooms, summoned like ghosts, to see what the smell was. I finished cooking my curry, made some basmati rice to go with it, and reluctantly offered some to my friends. They didn't get seconds. They got thirds. Cut to a year later, now I cook my stinky delicious food on s semi-regular basis, and my roommates have started adding curry powder to everything.

—ACHOL CHOWDHURY | BANGLADESH

I think the taste of home, for me, is anything my mom makes. Those flavors and combinations of spices, with the added love, is something I cannot find anywhere in the world. No restaurant ever comes close.

—ADITYA DIXIT | INDIA & NEW ZEALAND

The taste of home is spicy. There is nothing quite like the food in Indonesia. It's either sweet or spicy, and always unique. Other food in comparison is bland.

—KENISHA WARDHANA | INDONESIA

It is not part of the American culture to eat dishes like soups, and sometimes when I say I crave soup people think I'm sick because that's only time they eat soups here.

—DENITSA KANEVA | BULGARIA & NORWAY

For eighteen years of my life, breakfast has always been rice, lunch has always been rice, and dinner has always been rice. Then I moved to Australia where we eat toast or cereal for breakfast, sandwiches or salads for lunch, and pasta for dinner. My first year was full of me taking gastric pain medicine every day around lunch time because I was just so hungry, and bread doesn't fill me.

—CYNTHIA ARIELLA | INDONESIA

When people invite you to eat out, they don't mean come eat with them and they'll pay, it just means you're going for the company, but you'll still pay your own bill. This is fascinating for me because in my country, if I invite you out for anything, it's an automatic assumption because I am inviting you, I will pay for everything unless clearly stated well in advance.

—SHALOM WANYONI | KENYA

I find it interesting they came up with so many foods to eat with your hands like burgers, hotdogs, corn dogs, popcorn, and chicken wings, but God forbid you eat rice or anything else with your hands. I just don't see why anyone should be shamed for it.

—ALIA ALHADDAD | SAUDI ARABIA

I bought a pandan cake I found in the Asian store. I immediately bought it because I miss the taste of pandan sweets, and I brought it with me to go play some games with some friends. The cake was green, and apparently one of the people there found it disgusting. They kept repeating "ew, ew ,ew" for several minutes, and so eventually I had to wrap it up and save it for later.

—IVY DIGNITY | INDONESIA

.

She called the Tang Yuan disgusting right in my face, this dish which I so loved and gave me a sense of comfort while I was away from home. Every time I boiled some up, she'd pretend to retch in front of me and make these vomiting sounds. She'd call it gross, and it made me so mad. Yet, though I knew I had every right to cook it whenever I wanted, I couldn't help feeling self-conscious every time. I ended up constantly having to sneak in opportunities to eat it while she was out just so I could avoid having to deal with her reactions.

—ANONYMOUS | SINGAPORE

For a lot of people, college is an interesting place where the East and West meet each other for the first time as peers in an academic environment. In Singapore and Malaysia, when you see white people, there's a difference in power dynamics. To us it's like seeing a unicorn; they're the rare type of expats, and they're the experts brought in from out of town to do what our own people could not. When we enter university as international students, all of a sudden there isn't any of that difference in superiority like how we've always been made to perceive growing up back home. We start to see how they, too, come with their own flaws and struggles, just like we do. This is also often the first time both cultures actually get to know one another, because prior to this, many of us have only ever seen each other on screens or read about the other on paper, but now here we are mixing with one another as equals.

—RONNY CHIENG | MALAYSIA, SINGAPORE, AUSTRALIA, & UNITED STATES

CHAPTER 6

THE CULTURAL PARADIGMS OF EDUCATION

———

Featuring Ronny Chieng

CONGREGATION

There is more to culture shock than just the superficial changes of having to adjust to a new diet, get used to speaking a new language, or the little tangible things like using new vocabularies or modes of transportation. The challenge for international students coming into college is not only having to register that transition from being high schoolers to university students, but also trying to process the shock of having just moved to an entirely new country with an entirely different culture. The pressures to deliver outstanding academic performances, build an impressive resume, and figure out a career plan while also trying to maintain an active social life, get enough sleep, along with a myriad of other challenges for a college student become heavier under the weight of also having to navigate how to be a foreigner at the same time.

Never underestimate the international students' ability to quickly organize amongst ourselves. I go more in-depth with this discussion in the next chapter, exploring the reasons *why* international students from the same or similar national and/or cultural backgrounds tend to congregate so tightly with one another, but for now, let me tell you about the how—at least within the context of inside the classroom.

* * *

I remember standing outside the lecture hall with all the other students in my class waiting for our session to start. To my right were all the American students scattered around, mostly on their phones minding their own businesses, scrolling through social media, texting their friends, listening to music, or chatting with the person next to them. A bit further away to my left, were all the other international students who were congregating into their own separate national and/or cultural groups, establishing new connections with those they had just met or touching base with the people they probably coordinated to take the same class with since last semester. They would already be exchanging contact details and assembling group chats on WhatsApp, Facebook Messenger, LINE, KakaoTalk, or WeChat and planning study sessions, meetings to do assignments together, and discussions amongst ourselves.

Are we graded for participation and attendance? How many tests and quizzes do we have? Is the final cumulative? Does anybody have past papers, notes, or cheat sheets handed down to them they can share? Toward the end of the semester, or during one of the long breaks, you best believe I will be hearing from a couple of the Indonesian kids in my departments asking me which courses I'm taking for the next semester. *Which class session is it? Which professor is it? Are they an easy grader? Do you know any other Indo kids taking that class? Let's take it together!* Then sure enough, if I do end up in the same class as that one Indonesian kid the next semester, I end up in the same class as five or ten others who are all sitting together.

Me? I always stood awkwardly in the middle, trying to find where to walk the line between wanting to be independent enough to stand on my own and letting myself depend enough on a community to have a safety net to catch me in case I fall. Sometimes I'd like to sit with them in case either one of us needs the other's help, and other times I want to sit alone so I can just focus on myself. I prefer to sit in the middle or in the front of the class because *yes, I am one of those students* who likes to be the first to raise my hand to ask or answer questions. Indonesian students, on the other hand, are usually clustered together at the very back of the class or toward one side of the room to avoid getting called on by the professor.

For many international students, whether it's with those of your same nationality (e.g., Indonesians with Indonesians) or those of other foreign nationalities (e.g., Indonesians and Kuwaitis), forming these groups is essential because it provides the support and reassurance many of us need to feel safe and secure throughout the semester. We know we have each other to turn to and lean on when things are bound to get tough. It was often a relief to know I was not the only international student in a class because I just don't like to work alone. That's almost always the issue whenever I'm the only non-American kid there because eight times out of ten, American students tend to be a lot more individualistic and prefer to work and study by themselves. Since high school, I've always felt more comfortable completing assignments either with my teachers, a tutor, or in a study group with my classmates, mostly because I was afraid to get something wrong. It's not that we're too dependent or spoiled, it's that most of us come from cultures where we were never allowed to make mistakes. Unless we're absolutely confident we can get everything right on our own, we work as a team to prevent as much of those mistakes from happening in the first place, as mistakes do not ever simply go unpenalized.

As a Brazilian, I am used to being friends with everyone around me and helping everybody out with everything. In the American classroom setting, the students are there to do their own thing, and they usually do not talk to each other unless they really have to. Sometimes I have more than one class with the same person for an entire semester and we never talk, not even once.

—MARIANA VIGNOLI | BRAZIL

OUT OF PLACE AND OUT OF LINE

When I was still fresh off the plane from Indonesia, it took me a while to realize so many of the student habits I've had my whole life suddenly became so out of place in America. For a while, I was raising my hand to be excused to use the restroom during classes before realizing you could just get up and leave to go to the bathroom without permission. Classroom or campus dress codes were little to non-existent, but I guess part of that was largely just the culture of college itself. One moment you're passing by someone in a suit and tie looking like they're ready to take over Wall Street, and the next you see someone in their pajamas and furry slippers eating a breakfast burrito at twelve in the afternoon. I have seen men come to class in those gym tanks that *barely* cover anything, and women show up to class *very evidently* not wearing bras (#FreeTheNipple).

Whenever I was late to class, I'd send my professors long emails apologizing and explaining the reasons for my tardiness or stay back after class to explain myself in person, when they're just glad I even showed up in the first place. I've seen plenty of students casually arriving in the middle of the lecture *a whole ass thirty-minutes late,* and the professors neither penalize them for it nor questioned them for it in front of the entire classroom. One thing that always baffled me was how students could leave in the middle of a class with neither notice nor valid reasoning, while the professor is still teaching, simply because they were either too bored or had to tend to other commitments. I couldn't believe students were not getting punished for these kinds of behaviors left and right. At first, I was so used to Asian classroom discipline where all of these behaviors would have been considered extremely disrespectful toward the professor, and even to the rest of the class, for being disruptive. Mind you, this was my experience at my college; not all American colleges are like this, and not even *all* of my classes were like this.

It was harder to discipline myself when even my own professors weren't expecting us to be disciplined.

—TABITA CHRISTASSIA | INDONESIA

Respect toward elders and those of a higher position of power is also often an important cultural value that does not exist on the same level in many Western societies. This is not to say people in the Western world do not respect their elders, just that it's expressed differently. In tune with their individualist values, Western societies are low power-distance (LPD) cultures and are laxer when it comes to relationship dynamics between the young and old, between student and teacher. One key characteristic of many collectivist societies, on the other hand, is a high power-distance (HPD) culture where acknowledgment of hierarchical structure and ranking are customary if not mandatory—and this is standard across the board whether you're in school or university, at work, or even with your family and friends.

Once we move to college in the West, grade-hierarchy and age-hierarchy go straight out the window. It's not shocking to have a first-year dating a third-year or have a second-year be in the same friendship groups as fourth-years. Most college classes combine students from different grades, and even within those different grades, there could be different age groups. Some students could only be one grade above me, but three or four years older than me. Some students could be two grades below me, but the same age as me. Although they didn't make anything out of these differences, subconsciously it sometimes affected the way I formed acquaintanceships with students outside and inside of the classrooms—not because I wanted them to, but because they were old cultural habits that were hard for me to shake off. I tended to care about someone's grade more than I did their age. As long as they were two or more grade-levels apart from me, there was always a perceptible difference in power dynamics between us. If they were older, there was always that sense of needing to be more courteous and reserved around them. If they were younger, I personally didn't care as much, but sometimes there was pressure on me to be more confident around them and look like I knew what I was doing (even when most of the time I didn't).

More than anything, perhaps the most culturally shocking thing to me when I first got to college in America was how casual teachers and other adults were with their honorifics. Where I'm from, and this is also true of most HPD cultures, it's very important to address a person according to their appropriate titles to convey respect—especially when they're older. Not only was it acceptable for students to refer to professors by their first names, but some of my professors even preferred it. I had a few professors who rather I called them *Kathy* or *Alex,* even in class in front of the other students. I had some professors who were adamant about being referred to by their respective titles like "Doctor" or "Professor," but it seemed to me most of them didn't really care. It was more common for me to hear students refer to our professors as Dr. Gutierrez or Professor Elkinawy when addressing them in class but then refer to them as Angelica or Susan among other students, or even when talking to the teachers themselves outside of class. Somehow even my bosses felt more comfortable with me calling them Angelina and Kyle instead of Mrs. Lee and Mr. Kim-Greenberg.

I've noticed professors are quite chummy, especially with graduate students because we're considered their peers rather than students. It took me a few years (and also working in that department) to eventually feel the same way for my professors. In one of my earlier undergraduate years, one of my professors wanted me to call her by her first name, and I just couldn't do it comfortably all year. For a while, as an undergraduate student, it was quite awkward emailing professors because I didn't know how to address them—or rather, how formal I should be.

—TIMOTHY TAN CHIN GUAN | MALAYSIA & INDONESIA

It's also common in many colleges and universities in the anglosphere for students to form more intimate relationships with their professors (and no, I don't mean *that* kind of intimate relationship, although they probably do happen). Perhaps this was one of those special perks of going to a smaller, tight knit community school, but many students at LMU consider their professors to be just as much their friends as they are their educators. This was definitely true for me, which was something I loved and cherished about my college experience. There were times I would randomly swing by my professors' offices to talk about literally anything, for no reason other than I just wanted to, and they were always welcoming of it! It's not rare to find students and professor chatting over a cup of coffee at the campus cafe, and students even babysit at their professors' homes. In Asian cultures, on the other hand, respecting and fearing your teachers are considered synonymous. The idea of engaging with our educators outside of the classroom and outside of academic-related purposes is rare if not completely unheard of.

ATTENTION STUDENTS, CLASS IS NOW IN SESSION

Academia in the non-Western world is highly authoritarian and there is a lot of emphasis on discipline and following orders. Even as an undergraduate college student, so long as you're under the roof of an academic institution, there are rules you are expected to abide by and consequences for when you don't. Academia in the Western world, on the other hand, tends to give students ample space to do things the way they think is right for themselves. By the time you get to college in the West, you get an almost unlimited scope of liberty to do whatever you want, whenever you want. However, too much liberty can be overwhelming and leave some of us in a state of paralysis when we become unsure of how to navigate having that much freedom so suddenly. The lack of formal structure in Western classrooms can often be a jarring adjustment for international students coming from more conventional academic cultures where we're used to being kept on a tight leash by our educators. Despite growing up in more westernized education systems, I was no exception.

Participation and showing up to class make such a huge percentage of your grade, which blew my mind coming from Germany where attendance and participation are more on the voluntary basis. In America, they give so much homework, quizzes, and assignments. My university back home had like one to two assignments, or one assignment and one exam per semester per class, and you could take it up to three times.

—VALEA METZGER | GERMANY

A lot of things suddenly became optional—which classes to enroll in, how many classes to enroll in for the semester (so long as it hits the legal minimum of twelve credit hours for US international students), pen or pencil, handwritten notes or digital notes. Attendance was sometimes not graded, and homework and other assignments were sometimes voluntary submissions. Some classes didn't have final exams, just final assignments, and even then, some of those were made optional. Every time we were given a written assignment, I was that kid in class who raised her hand to ask what font style, size, and spacing we needed to use. *How many pages or words should we write? Do we need to indent the first line of each paragraph? Do we need a cover page? What citation style should we use, and how many should we include? Should we submit it as a word document or a PDF?* My first semester of college, I even emailed professors before tests and exams to ask if we were allowed to use whiteout or multicolored highlighters and pens. I'll never forget a professor's response when I asked him some of these questions for an essay assignment. He said, "Indah, you could hand write your paper on a piece of ripped, coffee-stained paper you got from the recycle box of the first-floor library. Write it to me in an email in whatever font style and size you want; leave a paper underneath my office door, I don't care. Just as long as you do the assignment, and it is legible."

You can call it being a nerd, dynsfunctionally anxious or just overly excessive, but a lot of the times that's just how scared I was of getting something wrong. I was so used to having someone give me detailed instructions of what exactly I needed to know, what I needed to do, or having someone check my work on the spot and telling me if I'm doing it right or not. I just don't come from a culture that has taught me to deal with uncertainties. I'm used to relying on clear and direct commands to follow, and when I no longer had any of that, it became difficult. It became even more difficult on top of my hyperawareness that I was possibly being a burden to my professors or being perceived negatively by other students who just didn't understand why I behaved this way.

THE CULTURAL IMPLICATIONS OF PEDAGOGY

Different cultural values of education not only impact students' methods of learning, participation, and engagement within the classroom, they also influence comprehension of concepts like hierarchy, equality, freedom, democracy, and the ways such ideas may be expressed inside the classroom. I should point out there could be a plethora of differences between international students and domestic students I would never be able to cover all in this one chapter alone, on top of the fact sometimes it's difficult to gauge which differences are attributable to differences in culture, or just the mere fact high school and university are inherently two completely different cultural systems of their own. Furthermore, keep in mind a lot of what I am about to say next is mostly based on my own experience in the United States, and may not be entirely applicable to other international students. That being said whether it was in a big lecture hall with a hundred other students, or in a small classroom with less than ten students, there were consistent patterns in the behaviors and tendencies shared amongst us international students that I would notice were very different than that of our American counterparts.

In Eastern culture, precision and accuracy are of the utmost priority. We would rather sacrifice a bit more time for the sake of achieving perfection than the other way around. The way I see it, this cultural disposition of being incredibly detail-oriented tends to manifest within the academic environment in two particular ways: note-taking and our style of working or learning.

I often noticed a slight distinction between the note-taking tendencies of international students and the American students. Please note I realize this is not all students, and

I have found no empirical research that can back up my hypothesis, so this is entirely based on my testimonial and should be taken with a grain of salt. That being said, I think it's less to do with *how* international students tend to take down our notes and more to do with *the amount* of notes we take down.

Note-taking can be categorized in two ways.[28] The first is generative, which pertains to summarizing, paraphrasing, and concept-mapping. The second is non-generative, which involves more verbatim duplication of information. The way I saw it, American students tend to be more of the former, while my international friends and I tend to be more of the latter, particularly the Asian (including Middle Eastern) students. In general, I saw a lot more American students who seemed to focus more on big picture concepts and who generally don't mind minor idiosyncrasies and inconsistencies so long as they get the job done, and they get it done either earlier, or right on time. This was possibly why, in my classes, it was rare to see an American student taking the time to copy down *every single word* on the board or lecture slide, unlike many of my international peers who, like myself, would usually be the ones to ask the professor to kindly go back to the previous slide.

Just as how international students tend to copy our notes verbatim, I noticed we have the tendency to memorize our notes verbatim as well. Now *this* has actually been proven by empirical research I found featured in the National Forum of Applied Educational Research Journal. Educational systems in many schools worldwide place heavy emphasis on

---

28 James Doubek, "Attention, Students: Put Your Laptops Away," *NPR*, Published April 17, 2016.

memorization and students' ability to be able to reproduce information exactly word for word according to textbooks and other resources. Western educational systems, on the other hand, are more concerned with students actually understanding the concepts or theories being taught, and then reproducing that same information in their own words. As a result, many international students often find tasks dealing with the need to do independent problem solving to be daunting, and often struggle to adjust to the educational system in the anglosphere, which relies more on exploration, analysis, and synthesis.[29]

* * *

Western education encourages students to be openly critical. The classroom is established as a safe space to debate and question everyone and everything, which is something I've personally always been comfortable with as someone who is naturally more outspoken and grew up in westernized academic settings. I didn't have an issue with challenging the opinions of peers and professors or being the first to raise my hand to ask or answer questions. On the other hand, although other exceptions to this exists, many if not most international students (at least in all of my classes at my school) were the complete opposite, but from a more cultural perspective, I've always understood why.

---

29 Marion B. Couvillion and Sue S. Minchew, "A Comparison of American and International Students' Lifestyles and Perceptions of the University Experience" *National Forum of Applied Educational Research Journal* No. 16, No. 3 (2003): 1-2.

*If participation means speaking, and non-participation means
silence, then instructors requiring participation are privileging
those who already have power.*

—STEPHANIE VANDRICK AT UNIVERSITY
OF SAN FRANCISCO'S DEPARTMENT OF
RHETORIC AND LANGUAGE.[30]

Education in other cultures encourages students to be
more compliant. Traditionally, they are not taught they have
the right to question what is being taught unless they've
reached a high point in their academic or vocational careers
to do so. Moreover, it comes back to the topic of respect for
our seniors and elders, which is demanded at all times rather
than given only when earned, like what is taught in Western
societies. Students tend to avoid being critical out of respect
for their teachers, their peers, and to preserve classroom har-
mony. There is also a culture of "losing and saving face" for
many of us. Losing face means to bring shame, and saving
face means to prevent shame. Students are more reluctant
to speak up against faculty, not only to save their professors
from losing face in front of the other students, but also to
prevent themselves from losing face and out of fear of being
ridiculed for asking questions or making statements viewed
as moronic or disrespectful.

*The way we were taught in Singapore, it was very much one
directional learning from the teacher to the student, so the idea
of being expected to participate was very daunting, and not*

---

30   Stephanie Vandrick, "Language, Culture, Class, Gender, and Class Par-
     ticipation," (2000).

something all students were prepared to do, or even saw the benefit in doing. I don't want to speak for other countries cultures because I didn't study in any other countries', so I don't mean to generalize, but I have observed that for people with Asian educational backgrounds specifically – that idea of volunteering an answer or admitting that you didn't understand what was going on, was just not something you would ever do. Even in law school in Australia, it was still very much rote learning with a little more interaction depending on the lecturer. The Socratic method of learning through speaking up and answering is very much an American thing only. In Singapore, students would generally consider the Socratic method to be a waste of time.

—**RONNY CHIENG**

We'll often hear from our professors, as a way to encourage us to speak up more in classes, "There is no such thing as asking dumb questions." Culturally, that sentiment does not register where a lot of international students are from. Whether it's been taught at school or at home by our parents and family, we're taught there *is* such a thing as asking dumb questions, so many of us will just avoid asking anything at all—again, out of fear of being ridiculed, or even getting into trouble. Unlike in Western cultures where making mistakes is seen as a valid—and even essential—part in all areas of learning, mistakes are considered highly unacceptable to the standards of most Eastern cultures. If you have ever wondered why so many international students, typically those from the East, are so reluctant to participate during classroom discussions in general, this is really one of the big reasons why. It's for the same reasons some tend to prefer sitting next to their own people, or at least huddle near one another in class, especially where they can also speak in their own language together. When they don't understand something, or know something, they don't ask the professor in front of the entire class. Instead, they'll ask each other. In some cases, they may even be too afraid to ask the professor alone after class or outside of class.

All of this has even been empirically proven by research. Reluctance in participation is often so much more than international students just being shy. In a research paper written by the aforementioned professor, they said "the way educators define 'participation' has both pedagogical and political implications for students, particularly for students who do not perceive themselves as being entitled, at least in the educational setting."[31] Silence in the classroom is a function of a significantly perceived power differential between parties.

The idea of the teacher asking a question, and a student saying something that could be the answer is irrelevant. We just want to hear from the teacher because they are the ones marking the paper and who ultimately determine what our grades are, so we'd rather just hear from them. Everything else was a waste of time. That was the mindset. I'm not saying that's the right mindset, but I'm saying those are the ideas we had going in. Some of that was cultural, and some of that was just part of transitioning into university where it's already a very different style of learning.

—RONNY CHIENG

---

31   Ibid.

Other important factors that are mentioned in the research that may affect student participation other than language, which I already discussed in the second chapter, are gender and social class. Are they female? Are they from working-class backgrounds? Belonging to both of these characteristics may also intensify the difficulties experienced by some students. Vandrick's study is accompanied by research showing how female students across a range of different ages are less likely than male students to speak up, especially when unsure of a correct answer or when uncertain of what they have to say.[32] For some international students, this too is a cultural implication. Many females come from more patriarchal cultures and are not only accustomed to seeing the works and opinions of our male counterparts valued more highly than ours but have also been raised to internalize that misogyny.

Coming from working-class backgrounds often correlates with being a first-generation college student, and while I do not come from the former background, I do come from the latter, hence this being something I empathize with. Students belonging to either one or both backgrounds often feel insecure about our participation—in all areas of college life really, not just during classroom discussions. We realize other students who come from more privileged family backgrounds may have more advantage over us. Considering the community I come from, I'm more often surrounded by other Indonesian students who are not only wealthy, but also have at least one parent or one older sibling who has graduated from college in the anglosphere before them, so it was a lot of pressure on me to always get everything right out of fear

32   Ibid.

my mistakes and shortcomings would not only be a reflection of *my* ignorance and inadequacy, but also that of my mom's.

RUBBER MEETS THE ROAD

Exploring the cultural paradigms of education within a multicultural academic setting could be an entire book or Netflix show of its own. There is so much more that could be said on this topic, but my intention with this chapter was to highlight some of what I thought were the main cultural differences and complexities of school etiquette most international students have to adapt to based off my own personal classroom experience, as well as those of my peers. Education is just as much cultural as it is political, and hopefully this chapter provided adequate introduction into understanding that. This was also the longest chapter in the entire book because I felt this topic ranked the highest, not just in terms of relevancy, but also in importance. I think the classroom is actually where the rubber meets the road within our academic journeys abroad. Our very status as international *students*, and purpose of being in the anglosphere, are literally and legally dependent on the condition that we sit in a classroom in the first place. In a sense, it's like our "assigned headquarters," and it's the center where all cultural exchange and interactions *have* to take place, whether we want it to or not.

As much as educators need to help us foster an inclusive learning environment, and domestic students need to show compassion and understanding, international students also need to pull our own weights in not only unlearning old conventions, but also being open to accepting new ones. Change is a flame intimidating to the touch, but it's an empowering feeling when we eventually warm up to the fire and realize it's not going to burn us but better us. We'll come out the other side of it much more adaptable, more resilient, and much stronger. Be inspired to learn from each other – domestic or international. Uplift one another. After all, there is a lot of trepidation that comes with being a college student in general, *and we're all in this debauchery together anyway.* Whether it's the domestic students who never strayed too far from home, or the international students who flew across oceans from thousands of miles away, every group or individual comes with their own special set of struggles that are different from everybody else's, and that is where the spirit of our solidarity is found.

We were all entering adulthood for the first time and being expected to suddenly grow up and make adult decisions, even though we're not really adults yet, and this was true whether you were international or local. International students probably had a little bit more of that because we didn't have family around us, so we didn't necessarily have this support network of a familial culture system to guide us through that. We all had our challenges. You can argue on who had more or less of what, but generally speaking, I think the similarities are we were all just a bunch of kids trying to figure it all out, and that's the commonality.

—RONNY CHIENG

*Back home, we have this saying "masuk bareng, lulus bareng,"
which means "we start together, we graduate together." Having
to go from that kind of a culture to a culture where suddenly
no one really knows each other, there's no sense of attachment
to one another, no real connection or relationship with the
people in your class, and you just do whatever you have to do
for yourself to graduate and then get the hell out of there—it
kind of sucks.*

—ANDRE PRAWIRA | INDONESIA

*American professors tend to explain everything in detail step
by step, and they are much more patient with the students who
are struggling to keep up or understand the lecture materials.
Chinese professors are typically not, unfortunately. In American universities there is this culture of buying textbooks, or
at least feeling like you have to. Chinese professors normally
do not tell students to buy textbooks unless it is absolutely
necessary because they don't want students to have to spend
more money.*

—DIAO HONG SU | CHINA

*I feel like, as international students, we are more okay with
sharing our work with one another. It's a totally understand-
able thing to come up to each other and ask to see the other
person's work so we can see an example of how they did something or get inspiration. I think with the Australian students,
we run the risk of making it seem as if we want to plagia-
rize their work when that's more often not the case. From my
experience, I've noticed international students tend to prefer
group work where we can share the workload and share the*

price, but Australian students tend to prefer to work alone where they can pull their own weight and have the reward all to themselves.

—CLARISSA MIRANDA TANTINA | INDONESIA

There were moments in Pakistan when the teachers would be angry because you would ask a question and they would literally beat you up in class for it. Going to school in Pakistan was almost like surviving every day from getting beat up by the teacher.

—SAMEED SIDDIQUI | PAKISTAN & UNITED STATES

One major thing is there are no clear expectations for you and your studies. The professor won't give you specific instructions of what to study, and usually they won't check on your learning process on a day-to-day basis, unless you take initiative. American professors usually have very strict office hours they set aside for students to come up to them with questions during that time, and only that time. Based on conversations with my Chinese friends, even in college, Chinese professors tend to be more attentive. They will take care of your studies for you, let you know exactly what you need to know, and directly ask the students if they have any problems or questions. Chinese professors are also reachable at any time, not just during office hours. They would usually give their personal contact information to students, which rarely happens in the US.

—JENNIFER CHEN XI | CHINA

Being in another foreign country can sometimes feel like we're in a perpetual state of anxiety, so often times it's important we have a community of people who we can revert back to when we are in need of something comfortable and familiar to keep us sane. There is power in being able to surround yourself with people who won't always question you and expect you to explain yourself for every single thing you do like you're being put under a microscope. You know they understand exactly where you are coming from.

—TEN FRANCIS | UNITED STATES, THAILAND, & CHINA

CHAPTER 7

BIRDS OF A FEATHER FLOCK TOGETHER

THE C-WORD

Back in college, I was talking to an American friend after class, recapping my weekend spent with a group of Jakarta friends. He then asked, "Oh God, are you one of those international students who only hangs out with kids from your country?" I told him I had a good mix of other international friends (Indonesian and others), as well as American friends – *clearly,* he was one of them. He proceeded, "That's good. I don't like that so many international students come all the way here to study in America but only want to stick amongst themselves. What's the point of coming here then?"

It's true birds of a feather flock together. We'll see a group of Saudi kids chatting amongst themselves on campus, the Taiwanese kids clustered together in one area of the lecture hall, a group of Indian students studying together at the library, and all the Nigerian students eating their lunch together at the dining hall. Indonesians make up the top three largest foreign nationalities at my school, and although most local students probably didn't know where the country is located, many were aware of our existence as a national community. I recall one day in class where I was having a conversation with an American student and she said to me, "All the Indonesian kids never like to talk to anybody else outside of their own little groups, and they usually all sit together at the back of the class. I'm surprised you're even one of them."

I can't say I've never thought the same way. Even amongst some of my close Indonesian friends, we would often criticize other Indonesian kids for their culturally exclusive tendencies. I should iterate there is nothing wrong about wanting to hang out with your own people. Humans have the natural psychological tendency to stick to those of the same cultural, religious, and political affiliations due to the likelihood of sharing similar values, beliefs, interests, and even for security.[33] That being said, there's a difference between a *community* and a *clique*. Of course, such entitlement exists amongst a few bad crowds of international students who choose to stay bubbled in their own closed-mindedness. However, I always had good faith that most international students are genuinely not like that at all, and despite what it may seem like to some of us looking in from the outside, deep down some of these students have legitimate reasons for why they do what they do. I wanted to put that faith to the test, which was why I wanted to hear what some of my participants had to say about this topic through surveys and interviews, and here are some of their responses:

---

33   Miller McPherson, Lynn Smith-Lovin, and James M. Cook, "Birds of A Feather: Homophily in Social Networks," *Annual Review of Sociology*, Vol. 27 (2001): 415.

I hung out with only Indonesian kids a lot of the times because I was too self-conscious about my English. It wasn't until I graduated from college and started working in a company where I was the only Asian that I started to break out of my shell and started hanging out with local coworkers. It's not that I didn't want to be friends with them, I really wanted to, but I think due to cultural differences and my introverted tendencies, I just didn't know how to approach them or initiate a conversation. I feel a sense of receptiveness and camaraderie from other international students. I don't think the responsibility to make friends with local students should be entirely all on us. The local students should also do their part on being informed on how to be more open and put in a bit more effort to get to know us.

—CLARISSA BOEDIARTO | INDONESIA

Sometimes I just get sick of having to constantly listen, learn, think, and talk only in English all day, every day. I need to be able to speak Russian with other Russian-speaking people to even continue functioning and feel sane. I have a whole different personality when I speak in Russian versus when I speak in English, and when I don't get to speak in Russian, it's like another part of me and my personality is missing. No matter how many local friends you have as an international student, even if you don't want to be around your own people, I think sooner or later you'll realize you actually need to have at least some of them around.

—VERONIKA PETROVA | RUSSIA

Despite the fact my international friends were not from the same country as me, I felt the cultural similarities overlapped more often than not, and empathy and advice came naturally and much more genuinely among us. The biggest barrier I had which prevented me from making domestic friends was I had to constantly serve as an educator or someone they could learn from when it came to racism, culture appropriation, and microaggressions, among other things. I am willing to teach someone, but it can't be my personal responsibility to be constantly correcting and teaching others about diversity and inclusion. That is not to say international students are exempt from those things, of course it happens amongst us too, but more often than not we are the minority and therefore always at the receiving end.

—SARITA CRUZ | HONDURAS

I see it as our biggest loss when we choose to forego opportunities to surround ourselves with people from different cultures—a privilege we know many people back home would kill for the chance to have but don't. However, one thing I've come to realize was having these kinds of opportunities right in front of you means absolutely nothing if you don't also have the ability to even seize them in the first place. Just because the tree is standing right in front of you doesn't mean you know how to grab the apples on top. *Heck, sometimes the tree does not even want to be approached.* So, just because you've had the privilege of being in countries like Canada, Australia, the US, or the UK doesn't mean you've had the privilege of knowing how to talk to the people there. It also doesn't necessarily mean all the people there want to talk to you all the time, either.

Sometimes I forget some people don't come from backgrounds where they grew up speaking English the way I did or had the knowledge and experience of interacting with different cultures like I've had. These things obviously matter when you're trying to branch out and make new friends who are different from you and everything you've ever known. Forming racial or ethnic groups within diverse multicultural settings is an automatic developmental process in response to environmental stressors, and not only do international students and their peers forget that, but educators and school administrations as well.

CLUSTERING

Back in high school, I often saw how when students of the same cultures got together, school administrators and students not only demanded an explanation as to why they did it, but wanted to know what could be done to prevent it. There was a *huge* Korean student population at my high school, most of whom would prefer to mingle among themselves both inside and outside of class and at other school related events and activities. This did not mean they were unfriendly toward non-Korean kids, many of them interacted with other people, too. However, they were occasionally reprimanded by certain faculty members and students who were under the impression they were contributing to segregation at a school that prided itself on its multicultural student body. At times it was hard to not agree with this sentiment, but a lot of the times I could sympathize with why the Korean kids stuck together.

Most of those Korean kids did not grow up in Indonesia or in other multicultural environments where they were already accustomed to interacting with different people. They were the average born-and-raised Koreans straight out of South Korea who went to Korean schools where everything was done in the Korean language. One day they came home and were told they needed to pack up their entire lives into boxes and suitcases, leave everything and everyone they've ever known and loved behind, and move to this random ass country they had probably never even heard of or seen on a map before. They were going to have to get familiar with an entirely new school system and try to learn a new foreign language when some of them had barely even gotten English down to begin with. All of this was in the backdrop of also trying to deliver outstanding academic and extracurricular results and trying to live up to outrageously high and demanding expectations from their parents at home.

They had all of these intentions that could sometimes get lost in translation because they were sometimes not linguistically articulate enough to convey their thoughts and opinions to others who didn't speak the same language as them. They had all these feelings and emotions they had neither come to terms with nor learned how to process by themselves, and yet they were being forced to answer to people who couldn't understand why they are always so closed off and quiet around other people. It's not that they were "racist" or they "didn't bother speaking English," they were anxious, stressed, and *probably scared out of their goddamn minds*. They wanted to be around those who both literally and figuratively could understand them because it was likely the only positive coping mechanism they knew how to fall back on. It's unfair to place such high expectations on every international student to immediately become these intercultural social butterflies overnight.

* * *

Countless studies provide evidence for how creating cultural
spaces for students provides more than just emotional and
mental benefits. They can yield strong positive influences
on their academic achievements as well. In an article called
"Why the Black Kids Sit Together at The Stairs" conducted by
Dorinda J. Carter, professor and chairperson of the Department of Teacher Education at Michigan State University,
found formal and informal same-race peer networks for
Black students in a predominantly white independent school
not only facilitated their adjustment to an environment
where they were often seen as outsiders, but also supported
these students' academic success and created opportunities
for them to affirm their racial identities.[34] For international
students, however, it goes beyond just aspects of race.

Amongst *most* international students, there is that extra
layer of connection where it's not just a matter of not being
white, but also being people from non-English-speaking
countries as well. There is that level of mutual understanding
of exactly what it's like to be brought up in a world that has
always taught us to view the intersection of being both white
and native English-speaking as higher up on the racial and
linguistic pedestal. We experience camaraderie in how we
are all walking through the spaces of predominantly white
and English-speaking college campuses together in real
time. International students as a collective group are almost
always the minority in that we're foreigners, and minorities
will always be overpowered by the prejudices and biases of

---

34   Dorinda J. Carter, "Why the Black Kids Sit Together at the Stairs: The
     Role of Identity-Affirming Counter-Spaces in a Predominantly White
     High School," *The Journal of Negro Education* Vol. 76, No. 4 (2007): 542.

whoever is the majority—in this case, the domestic students (regardless of race). Even when our majority counterparts are not directly perpetrating acts of discrimination or contributing to a hostile environment, it's simply that they are unprepared to respond to us and our needs in ways that are sufficient or even suitable. This is why we turn to one another, whether it's other international students in general or the people from our same cultural background, for the support we want or need. The result of this often comes in the form of ethnic clustering within campus spaces.

Between us and our American-born POC counterparts, there was a sense of camaraderie in the fight for diversity, yet there is a quiet divide in knowing they have the privilege of a sense of clarity when it came to planning for life up to graduation and beyond. With the international kids, it's the collective lamentation of how do we apply for a visa, how do we sustain ourselves when we can't work the same jobs on campus, and how are we going to qualify and get a job that will sustain us after campus?

—NATASHA AQUINO | PHILIPPINES & SRI LANKA

UNITY IN DIVERSITY

The anglosphere is a native English-speaking, white-majority population. Whether you are an international student or a domestic student, I think there is solidarity there in terms of our ability to relate as, to put it simply, *"people of color."* I can relate to my Black American friends and Hispanic/Latino American friends on the basis of being racial minorities in the US. My Asian American friends and I do share some similar experiences here and there on the basis of being

Asian in general. That being said, that's really all there is to it. Personally, the focus of my international student experience in America had never been so much about *race*, or the fact I was not white, but rather about the fact I was just not an American. I didn't have that same citizenship or permanent resident status to provide the same kind of opportunities as my American friends. I didn't always have the same knowledge of American politics or history to help me understand certain cultural references in class, and I didn't always want to talk about news or socioeconomic and political issues only relating to America (or other countries in the anglosphere at best).

For the record, I'm not saying race wasn't an important factor in my experience because the very content of this book says otherwise. Race mattered, but my point is that it wasn't the only thing that mattered, and it wasn't the thing that mattered *all the time*. I think for many international students, whether you're from Kazakhstan, Switzerland, Myanmar, Ghana, or Uruguay, and regardless of whatever race you are, it is that foreigner status we hold collectively when we are there in the anglosphere that is the root of our commonalities. Being a foreigner, and especially being a foreigner from a specific country, is perhaps what most of us perceive to be the main defining aspect of our identities that shapes our experience of being there. Coming to America, I realized sometimes Americans saw me and my other international friends in a different context. A lot of the times it felt like the focus was less on the fact I was specifically from Indonesia, or I was specifically Chinese Indonesian, and more on me just being Asian.

When we go there, we see them as Americans, Canadians, Australians, or Brits, but they only see us for our color.

—ANONYMOUS | INDIA

People typically assume I'm a white American just because I'm white-passing, when I'm actually half-Chinese and was born and raised in Paris, France. In America, I think there is this tendency to think diversity comes from just the color of your skin, but I could be in a room with another dude who pretty much looks exactly like me and our experiences would be completely different.

—KEA BREAKMAN | FRANCE

It's in the little things, like how people simply ask me "What's Asia like?" as if all of Asia is somehow the same, or randomly mention an Asian country they've travelled to for the holidays after I tell them I'm from Indonesia, or when they think one particular Asian country's customs or traditions apply to all of us. *(The classic "Do you eat dogs?" question I swear everybody of Asian descent gets, which—let's not even get into that.)* I had a coworker who was showing a comedy video where some parts of the dialogue were spoken in *Tagalog*, and she asked *me* to translate. I told her I'm not Filipino and she asked, "But don't you guys speak the same language?" *We don't.* Another day I ran into my, at that point, former Vietnamese American roommate (yes, that same one) on campus who asked me if I went back to Malaysia for the holiday. I reminded her I'm from Indonesia, then she laughed and said, "Whatever, same thing!" I understand often times they're not coming from a bad place, and they just don't know any better, but it's infuriating and even degrading to oversimplify Indonesian, Singaporean, Korean, Taiwanese, or Cantonese people as being tantamount to Filipino, Malaysian, Thai, Chinese, or Vietnamese people just because we're all Asians and we're perceived to "look the same" or "sound the same." Just because people are part of the same *racial group* does not mean every *ethnicity* within that group goes through the exact same experience or share the exact same commonalities.

Another memorable experience I have with this was when I had told a white American friend I was planning to rush for the business fraternity I had talked about in earlier chapters. Without me telling him which fraternity it was, he had guessed the name of it correctly. I asked him how he knew, and he said, "Yeah, no shit, that's where all the Asians rush." I raised an eyebrow and asked, "Asian, or Asian American?" I already knew from my other friend who was a brother in that fraternity that it was mainly Asian Americans, but I just wanted to hear my friend's response. He said, "I'm not sure… I mean, does it matter? You're all still Asian." Respectfully, I beg to differ. There are aspects of the Asian American (or even Asian Canadian, Asian Australian, and British Asian, really) experience that not all Asians will necessarily relate to, and vice versa. The same can be said about Africans, Caribbeans, Europeans, Polynesians, Hispanics, Latinos, and their anglosphere equivalents. Most, if not all, cultures around the world often place a great deal of pride and significance toward their identity as independent countries, or as individual cultures distinct from any other, so to come to countries like America where all of that is suddenly just reduced down to skin color or other shared physical features is a *bit of an experience.*

Yes, I still remember not understanding the terms "something-American" like African American or Asian American. I was confused for so long, and then later I learned race was something else in the US, something much more complicated. I remember taking a US culture class in my ESL program, and they were teaching us how to say "people of color" instead of "colored people." I was just so confused and interested in why it was so hard for Americans to just be Americans.

—ISABELLA BRASCETTA GUERRA | VENEZUELA

I get particularly concerned when British-born people of color fail to understand the concept of ethnicity, citizenship, and nationality. They're British because of the fact they're born in the UK, but they're, for example, Indian due to their heritage, which is their ethnicity. One of my closest friends is Malaysian by citizenship and nationality, but she's Chinese by ethnicity. One time, she was with another Malaysian friend whose ethnicity is Indian. A person the two of them encountered together could not fathom how two people of two different ethnicities could be from the same country, while that person—an Indian British person themselves—lives amongst Black British, white British, Chinese British people, and so on.

—RAUWA KHALEEL | THE MALDIVES & MALAYSIA

In a way, I feel like this was the disconnect between many of the domestic students and the international students when looking at the topic of race and ethnicity, but from a historical standpoint, I understand why. It's an inherent cultural value that comes with being from these giant melting-pot countries of literally all different races, ethnicities, and even religions that, regardless of whichever one of those walks of life we came from before we got here, consider us all one and the same once we arrive. In the context of immigration and going there to adopt a new nationality, I get it. At the same time, there is such a heavy pressure for everybody there to live up to the value of equality by coming as close to the literal definition of the word as possible that it has created this culture of being afraid to see color. For the record, this isn't just happening in America or the anglosphere. I think this idea of colorblindness is starting to pick up in other countries around the world as well, and that, to me, is concerning.

I come from an immigrant family background. I grew up in international schools that had representations of different cultures and nationalities from all over the world. I was raised in a country whose official motto *Bhinneka Tunggal Ika* literally translates to the subtitle of this section. Not only is diversity a sentiment that has inherently followed me my entire life, it's been the culmination of all of these experiences that has gifted me the ability to see color, not as something that detracts from the world by making it more divisive, but as something that adds to it by making it more colorful. *It's okay to see color,* it's how you choose to see or react to color that matters. Equality doesn't mean everybody should be the same so nobody is treated different; it means valuing everybody the same even though we can see what makes us different.

Contrary to the title of this chapter, birds of a feather are actually not the only ones who flock together. Birds of several different species also flock together, one of the reasons being a mixture of different species can take advantage of different abilities.[35] As humans, we are really no different. We also benefit from our differences when we use them to pick up new languages, learn about cultures and societies, gain new global perspectives, and see the world through multicolored lenses. All of the friends, neighbors, and people I grew up with all my life have mostly been those of different ethnicities, nationalities, and those who speak different languages and practice different religions than mine. Throughout my college years, I've had the joy of calling Americans and other international students of every race, sexual orientation, and even political affiliations some of my closest friends to this day. The strength of all those friendships and relationships has always rested on the fact that we can bond in the things we share and learn from the things we differ. ***We have pride in the things that make us different, and solidarity in the things that make us similar.*** Don't victimize your differences. Embrace them and honor all of the different shades and hues that make you, *you.*

---

35   Paul R. Ehrlich, David S. Dobkin, and Darryl Wheye, "Mixed-Species Flocking," Stanford University, March 12, 2021.

I'm Chinese American, my best friend's ethnicity is Indian Portuguese from Hong Kong. My friend group includes people who are half-Irish half-Saudi, British Ghanaian, Indian, German-born Vietnamese, French, and so on. It's a diverse group, and I'm proud to learn from them as much as they learn from me. We never know what's going to happen when we blend our cultures together, but it's magical.

—ERIC C. WU | UNITED STATES

I find value in hanging out with my American friends just as much as my international friends, but I also feel like over time, unless you are able to adapt to the way they live their lives—in terms of daily habits or other shared activities like eating out or partying—it's a bit hard to find a sustainable common ground in the long run. At the end of the day, I always end up falling back to the people I grew up with, or those who come from more or less the same upbringing as me.

—DAVID KUSUMA | INDONESIA

I didn't have difficulties with other international kids, but I did have difficulties mixing in with the white, Black, and Hispanic Americans. We tend to not share a lot of common cultural interests. At least with Asian Americans, even without those things, there were still common points where we could connect due to coming from similar cultural backgrounds. Not to mention, there was the uncomfortable feeling of needing to be vigilant of accidental or not-so-accidental racism, so I guess around these groups I kind of did have my guard up all the time, which made it harder to connect with them.

—EDUARDO EDISON | INDONESIA

I think intercultural friendships are very hit-or-miss. When I was a sophomore, I lived with three other domestic students, and they seemed to just always have a lot of secrets that needed to be hidden from me. Whenever I tried to join in on their conversations, even if it was something I knew about, they always said, "Oh it's nothing, it's just hard for you to understand," or "I don't think you'd even like to party, Asians seem more introverted." On the other hand, my fraternity has a bunch of locals, and yet I was always included in their stories. It all just depends on the dynamics of that group and whether or not the people in it are open to different cultures.

—JENNA NGUYEN | VIETNAM

I didn't feel included at all within the Indonesian communities I was a part of. I think as international students abroad, especially those of us part of the cultural organizations at our universities, the question is how do we make sure those spaces actually serve the people they're being created for? These spaces are meant to be inclusive, but sometimes don't actually end up being that way, so how do we make sure everybody feels included?

—BISHKA Z. CHAND | INDONESIA

Having friends from different parts of the world adds so much to the people involved in that friend group. There is a constant exchange of cultures, and it really broadens everyone's worldview. One of the biggest culture shocks of coming to America, for me, was seeing how my American friends behaved around their parents—for example, calling them by their first name, getting away with having an attitude, etc. The first time I needed to call a friend's parent by their first name, I was terrified!

—BEYZA NAZLI YILMAZ | TURKEY

THE POLITICS OF LIVING IN BETWEEN

(warning, I get really *feelsy* here)

During the summers I would move, everyone typically has already left that place because of summer vacation, so it's hard to get that last moment in for goodbyes and closure. On the last day of school, I don't think most people really take in that it is the last time I'll see them. I don't think I take it in because it's easier to accept maybe I'll see them sometime later down the line. Instead of closing the relationship and saying goodbye, it just becomes this awkward situation where the relationship lasts a little longer because we talk on social media for a bit, but then it just ends up dying out on its own after some time. There really hasn't been any closure with anyone I've ever said goodbye to.

—AARON CROWLEY | TAIWAN, UNITED STATES, CHINA, & CANADA

CHAPTER 8

RELATIONSHIPS IN TRANSIT

——

EXPIRATION DATES

No textbook can teach you how to say goodbye to your friends, and it doesn't get any easier no matter how accustomed you've gotten to doing it. No number of prayers, meditations, or therapy sessions can help you reconcile with the fact you'll likely never get to see them ever again, and on the off chance you do, things will already be too different. If friendship in an international setting is difficult, dating and marriage are almost *impossible* when most of the world still comes from customs where not only are monocultural romantic relationships the societal norm, but they're also the expectation set by our parents. This does not yet even include, among many other things, the part of deciding where in the world the both of you would permanently reside for the rest of your lives. Who out of the two of you is going to have to give up their life in one country for the sake of their partner's life in another, lest the both of you decide to embark on the journey to move to a completely new and foreign country together—and that's even if both your families agree to it in the first place? Technological advancements—namely free messaging platforms, social media, and video calling—have definitely made long-distance relationships much easier, platonic or not. Nevertheless, it remains a struggle to frequently stay in contact, keep the sparks of the relationship alive, or have the friendship feel the same way it once did, when on top of being separated by land and sea, you're also being separated by the sun and moon.

Friendships at international schools come with expiration dates, time-limits pre-determined by the terms and conditions of employment contracts and work-visas on how much time expat students and their parents had to stay in the country before having to relocate to the next one their company was sending them off to. When I was in the fourth grade, I befriended this new girl in class who had just moved to Jakarta from Seoul, and who happened to live in a different building of my apartment complex. We went to school together in each other's cars in the morning. When we came home together, she'd come over to my place to eat my mom's spaghetti, or I'd go over to hers to listen to music. One day, toward the end of fifth grade, she told me she and her family were leaving Indonesia for good, *and I just lost it.* It was too much to process how one day my best friend who I had spent nearly every day with for the past year was just suddenly going to disappear without any explanation that was comprehensible to my 11-year-old brain.

Every year since, it was the same shit on repeat. Back in high school, we had an annual tradition where, during the last general assembly of the school year, they would call all of the students and faculty members who were leaving to stand in front of the entire school as a way to sort of say their final goodbyes. There was never a year where I didn't see someone I knew standing up on that stage, wishing they didn't have to leave. I think it made me grow up a little too fast for it to have been healthy. It's a very sobering experience for someone so young to have to think about how *every time* they make the decision to be emotionally invested in anyone, they're just going to end up leaving in a few years with little to no chance of ever seeing them again in the future, *and this is why now I have attachment issues and separation anxiety.*

I have found being left is harder for me than leaving, I think it's because I'm so used to the latter. I try not to make promises to keep in touch. I think people genuinely mean it when they say it, but few people realize at the time how much effort it can take, and most people lose steam eventually. I like to write people letters or notes because I don't want to feel like anything is being left unsaid.

—SARAH O'MALLEY GRAHAM | SINGAPORE

Perhaps to some people, I was asking for it. All my life, I relished in the fact I went to schools with such diverse student bodies, and that my own friend groups were an extension of that diversity. I always preferred forming relationships and acquaintanceships with students from other cultures over those from my own. Part of it had to do with how much I used to resent the Chinese Indonesian community, especially in high school. The other part had to do with simply wanting to take advantage of my international background to broaden my horizon. The US is so ethnically diverse, and I thrived in that. I took pride in the fact I had friends of every background, and I was never one of those international students abroad who only hung out within their own culture. I did not trap myself in a cultural echo chamber of recycled ideas and opinions. However, it was the first summer after moving away that I came back to Jakarta and realized most of the friends I had from both high school *and* college at that time were literally *everywhere else* but Jakarta.

Many international students come from cultures where there is still a strong preference toward forming homogamous relationships in terms of ethnicity, religion, and culture. In my experience, this has been true in both friendships *and* romantic relationships, which I will talk about in much greater depth in the next chapter, so brace yourself for *that* emotional rollercoaster. All of high school, my mom would always say to me, "Don't you have *other* friends?" By that she meant *other* Indonesian friends. It's not that she hated the non-Indonesian ones or even discouraged those friendships, she just wanted me to have at least some Indonesian friends. Part of it was she always held the opinion other friendships were perhaps not as worthwhile maintaining or putting much effort into if they are not with *your own people*. To her, sharing the same homeland and culture provided more palpable insurance to gauge the longevity of those relationships. Although I frequently ignored her, deep down I always understood where she was coming from and saw the validity in her logic. I remember one day she told me, "All of these friends you currently have, they won't be here forever." Fast forward a few years later, and she was right.

For many of the friends I graduated high school with, their time in Indonesia was up for good once they grabbed their diplomas and went off to college while their parents relocated to other countries. For some, however, their parents still had about a year or two left in the city, which meant they would likely be returning to Jakarta for the next two to three winter or summer breaks. Those two to three breaks eventually flew by. I came home the next summer, after my sophomore year, and the hard reality I had been in denial of acknowledging my entire life finally hit me like a truck. *Maybe mom was right on this one.* Maybe I should have put in more effort to have at least some local friends who also lived in Jakarta, and I was scared that perhaps it might have been too late, because now I'm sitting there face-to-face with the possibility that I might not actually have *anyone* here in this city once I eventually have to move back for good.

Back in high school, I was primarily friends with students who were from different countries. I always thought I should use what limited amount of time I have in college to connect with people from various other backgrounds. Now, I wish I had put in more time and effort into making more Indonesian connections because, at the end of the day, I'm going to be living in Indonesia. I wish I had gone to more of the Indonesian Student Association meetings and events at my school over these past few years, made the time to hang out more with my Indonesian friends and figured out a better balance between all of my social groups.

—DIANDRA TJOKROSAPUTRO | INDONESIA

At least when I graduated high school, it was never a concern whether or not I'd ever come back to Jakarta. Whenever I thought of the day I'd have to finally pack up my things and leave America for the last time, it *was* a genuine concern whether or not I'd be able to return to LA. Even while I am writing this book, it is still a concern, especially in the midst of the COVID-19 pandemic. *Sure,* maybe not *"ever,"* but definitely within the near future. All my life, I was always the one asking friends who were moving (or have moved) away when they would come back and visit Jakarta, and now it was my turn to be on the receiving end of that, and I realize now it's not always such an easy question to answer. I'd get messages from friends back in LA asking when I'll be back; international friends from other parts of the world asking when I'll be able to visit them in Shanghai, Manila, Mumbai, London, Berlin, or Saudi Arabia. The sad truth of it is *I just don't know.* I don't know when I'd be able to return, and how much of the factors that would allow me to do so are within my control. Obviously, I need time and money to travel. What if I only have one but not the other? *Shit, what if I don't even have both? How long would it stay that way? The next five years? Ten years? Forever?*

BELONGING IN BETWEEN

I think more than anything else, the reason why some international students like me struggle to find belonging within our own ethnic communities is because we tend to be the *"in-betweens."* It's not just me, it's a common trend I've seen with kids from other cultures who grew up in international schools in other countries as well. The Hong Kong kids are not *entirely Hong-Kongese,* the Indian kids don't always get along with the other Indian kids, and the Singaporean kids would rather hangout with the non-Singaporean kids most of the time. The Emirati kids prefer to speak in English but would sometimes throw in some Arabic, and the Chinese kids prefer to speak in Mandarin but would sometimes throw in some English. Whatever it is, it's like we're never wholly anything. We're always floating in the middle of everywhere but never exactly fitting in anywhere either. If you want the crass and not-so-politically-correct way of putting it, *we're a bunch of westernized eastern kids, or white-washed non-white kids.*

For how much I couldn't wait to get out of Indonesia after high school, moving away ended up becoming the very thing that taught me just how much I actually needed people from back home to keep me rooted to home while I was the furthest away I've ever been. But for me to find an unadulterated sense of belonging within the Chinese Indonesian community, or any community for that matter, required more than just superficial common interests and mutual amicability if we were to become anything more than just friendly acquaintances. Eventually, I did find what I called "my little pieces of home" in the small group of Indonesian friends I managed to make throughout those four years of college. Whether they were old friends who I went to high school with and rekindled our relationships while we were abroad, or new friends I'd met more recently in the US, we connected because we were "not like the other Indo kids." We knew what it was like to float specifically in between the spaces of both *"I'm not that Indonesian"* and *"I'm not that American."* We were all a little different from the rest of the crowd, and that's exactly what we embraced about one another.

Even though we did our own things, branching out into different groups and communities in search of experiences and perspectives that shaped us into our own individuals, we still yearned for a community we could lean on and the familiar comforts of the place we all came from. There was never any of that pressure to speak in any particular language, but there was no shame in mixing too much of both either. It's nice we understood each other in both the American/Western *and* Indonesian/Eastern cultural contexts we would have otherwise needed time and energy to explain to others. Above all else, these were *my* people (literally and figuratively) who I knew when the inevitable time came where I finally had to say goodbye to my life in Los Angeles, at least I'd still have them to come back home to.

THE MANY COLORS OF MATRIMONY

A controversial topic that tends to be the focus of many conversations surrounding intercultural relationships is about racial or ethnic preferences—especially within the context of dating. Where does *having a preference* begin to cross the line of *having a fetish?* How much of our preferences are reflective of certain internalized racisms? How much of the stereotypes and misconceptions harbored by international students affect who we choose to befriend and date? I found a study on cross-racial and cross-cultural dating preferences among Chinese, Japanese, and Korean college international students in the US by Dr. Zachary S. Ritter that presented some very intriguing results about this. Thirty-five out of the forty-seven interviewed participants (74.4 percent) reported they would ideally date someone from their own cultural background to prevent communication gaps as a result of language barriers. However, when removing communication from the equation, the international students appeared to have a racial hierarchy for their dating preferences. "Students were not only influenced by parental approval of dating partners, but also US media images that helped create a racial hierarchy of dating and cultural capital. White Americans were the most desirable dating partner, Asian Americans were slightly below white Americans, while African American, Latino, and Southeast Asian students were the least desirable."[36]

This might be an unpopular opinion, but I think it's okay, and even normal, if you generally prefer to date certain racial or ethnic groups over some others. I like tea better than coffee, but if it's really good coffee, then why the fuck not? However, a *preference* and a *condition* are two different things. I don't think it's okay to condition yourself to *only* date certain racial or ethnic groups and exclude others entirely. I remember I had a Korean friend in the ninth grade who had a crush on a white Canadian girl in his PE class. One day he confessed to her after class, and she responded, "Sorry, I don't like Koreans." In my opinion, that's just being a *racist asshole*. On the other hand, my first boyfriend in high school was a white guy who, in the middle of discussing this very topic, revealed to me his *list* of racial dating preferences, *chronologically numbered*. I wasn't too pleased to see how the progression of the racial groups, ranked from best to worst, also just so happened to go in order of fairest to darkest—to which he defended by saying while cultural proximity played a factor, physical assimilation by means of having similar skin-tones was also important to him. *Racist asshole?* Perhaps. It's a very poor example of acceptable reasons to have racial/ethnic preferences, but at the end of the day, people *are* entitled to be attracted to whoever they want, no matter how shallow or bigoted the reasons may be.

---

36 [1] Zachary S. Ritter, "Taboo or Tabula Rasa: Cross-Racial/Cultural Dating Preferences amongst Chinese, Japanese, and Korean International Students in an American University," *Journal of International Students*, Volume 5, Issue 4 (2015): 405-419.

Also, if you're wondering where I ended up on the list, I was third or fourth. *The caucasity of this bitch, I swear.*

For many international students, we grow up living within diverse settings which give us the exposure to become accustomed and tolerant of people from different backgrounds. It predisposes us to the belief that love, whether for friend or for partner, *should* be blind to color, culture, religious beliefs, and even wealth, gender, and sexuality, so long as it is what makes us happy and content. In a way, this programs us to adopt more *unconditional* orientations toward intercultural relationships where, although we may display romantic inclination toward some groups more than others, we're still open to any and all people. Our parents, on the other hand, have been primed to adopt more *conditional* orientations of intercultural relationships, where inclination toward any group is seen as conditional upon (amongst many other things) racial, cultural, and religious compatibility. While the trajectory of heterogamous relationship rates within the anglosphere have been on the upswing in more recent years, interethnic and interracial romantic relationships are still harder to embrace by the older generation in other cultures.

THE WHAT-IFS AND WHAT-COULD-HAVE-BEENS

Even without the clash of values between you and your parents, international dating is inherently difficult for other more obvious reasons. All of my past relationships have failed because either they moved away, or I moved away. That's not even including all the *what-could-have-beens* because we would rather forego any chance of ever *officially* being together than to go through the whole process of entering a long-distance relationship and waiting for the sparks to naturally die out overtime. As I grow older, I begin to think about how perhaps it would be a more logical and emotionally cost-efficient idea to just invest in finding someone who is also from the same city. It's simply much easier when I know Jakarta is where I'd likely be spending the rest of my life. *Save me all that long-distance relationship bullshit, cause these hoes ain't **that** loyal.* That was a joke, but in all seriousness, distance just *does* take such a toll on a relationship, no matter how much you two love each other and make time to talk and text with one another.

Two people can really love each other, and somehow it still isn't enough. In my opinion, long-distance relationships *between disciplined couples* could work if there is a realistic end goal, and you know the relationship has the means to eventually get there. Determining that end goal can be hard when some of us don't even always know where in the world we might end up within the next few years, what with most of us having tentative plans for careers or higher education like master's and doctorate programs. If you're from an expat family where your parents are still working for companies that may or may not relocate them to different countries every few years or so, that further complicates things, too.

If I had stayed in Italy, specifically in Florence, I would still have my high school best friends by my side. For three years, their absence made me feel awful. After moving abroad, getting back together with that group seemed less of a reality as the months went by. I tried to embrace the fact their departures were lessons, and some people are just not meant to be in my life anymore. Saying my goodbyes always worries me, but I've been so used to it. There's no other way to cope other than to

just accept perhaps the journeys we embarked on were the best
decisions we could have made at that moment.

—GIULIA BALDINI | ITALY

Not only that, but where in the world the two of you will settle down once you've passed the long-distance phase is not always a mutual agreement between international couples either. My Indian ex-boyfriend had every intention of acquiring citizenship in the US and spending the rest of his life there post-graduation. I did not. Even if I did, *I could not,* and I know it's too much to ask of *any* future partner to give up their life in another country to move with me to mine. Sad fact of the matter is there is objectively nothing—neither politically, economically, or even socially—appealing about moving to a country like Indonesia unless you're already from there to begin with, especially if your other options are realistically much better.

A LOVE SO WORTHY

A word of advice? Try not to think about it too much. That might sound stupid considering I went on about it for an entire chapter, and now it's probably all you are thinking about, *but really.* We are lucky we are a generation of internationals living in this new age of technology where the future of travel is not only becoming safer and more reliable, but also becoming more financially accessible. It's the only tangible fact that has allowed me to feel at peace with the fact that I may always have to be worlds away from so many of those I love. I know my goodbyes are never fully permanent. They're mostly temporary, however long that impermanence is. Sometimes all it really takes is one text message, one video call, or one plane ticket to realize some friendships *are* able to withstand the test of time and distance, that you could go multiple days, weeks, months, or even years without talking or seeing that person, and when you finally do, it's as if nothing's changed. As cheesy as it is, love *is* worth the fight. Some love *is* worth crossing oceans and climbing mountains for, no matter how long it's going to take, or whether or not our parents agree, which brings me to the next chapter.

I find it really nice to see how my friends grew up as they left to different places, ventured out in life, and flourished with their passions. It makes me feel kind of like a mama bird seeing her flock finally flying out of their nest. My favorite moments are when we catch up with each other, and I see how far they've gone! It may be as simple as me knowing how spoiled they grew up and seeing they now actually know how to do their own laundry.

—TEGISHTHA ANDHIKA IMAN SOEWARNO | INDONESIA

My biggest culture shock coming to America was the men here. They're not gentlemen. I remember this one guy had asked to exchange Snapchats with me, and then he messaged me and asked, "Hey do you want to link up?" I didn't really know what that meant, but I just assumed he wanted to hangout, so I said okay, and he told me to meet me at the lobby of his dorm. When I got there, he saw me, and then immediately signaled me to follow him up to his room. In the elevator I asked him "Did you forget something?" and he was like, "What? No?" So I asked him, "Then why are we going upstairs?" He said, "I thought you wanted to fuck." I've known him for five minutes! I was so shocked, and I just left right after that.

—VERONIKA PETROVA | RUSSIA

CHAPTER 9

THE BEST OF BOTH WORLDS

HOMECOMING

Growing up in international schools put me in a position where I was constantly exposed to westernized notions of love, family, and adulthood at school, only to then come home and realize that was just not my reality culturally. All my life it made me question whether or not I could ever mirror even just a little bit of what my Western friends had with their parents, in the context of my own family dynamics at home with my own mom. When I finally had the physical and mental space away from my mother to be my own person and think about who I wanted to be for myself, I had to also think about how I would reconcile that with who I have to be for her when I returned home. As internationals from non-Western backgrounds who often operate within westernized spaces, there is often shame in feeling like we are compromising our own cultural values for another—especially in the context of being at home with family. In a movement where more people of color are now reclaiming our own heritage, we're also faced with the question of how much of that heritage we want to reclaim as opposed to reform. If we are not willing to reclaim all parts of it, and are only willing to accept the parts that are acceptable and convenient to us, then to what extent are we just appropriating our own culture?

International students who end up adopting more westernized notions of love, romance, and family structuring often find it difficult to come back home to families and societies still largely preserving old traditional values of courtship and marriage. Different cultures have different standards on what age is acceptable to start developing romantic attractions and enter romantic relationships. Westerners usually begin exploring different romantic relationships by dating during their adolescence years. This is not only customary, but commonly encouraged by the parents as well.[37] *My Asian ass wasn't even allowed to so much as **think** about boys back in high school,* so to be surrounded by Western kids my age whose parents were *totally fine* with them bringing home their significant others, going on dates, and even traveling together either alone or with their families made me feel so out of place.

By the time we graduated high school, our expectations from our parents varied. Personally, my mom was never the type of parent to pressure me into dating or marriage, always encouraged me to take my time both throughout and after college, and for that I will always be grateful. What was most common among my circle of international friends (mostly Asians) was them having to go from not even being allowed

---

37   Kathrine Bejanyan, Tara C. Marshall, and Nelli Ferenczi, "Romantic ideals, mate preferences, and anticipation of future difficulties in marital life: a comparative study of young adults in India and America," *Frontiers in Psychology*, Vol. 5 (2014): 2.

to *stare* at members of the opposite gender for longer than two seconds all their lives up until high school, to suddenly having to bring home a future husband or wife as *soon as possible—preferably before graduating university.* There was often a heavier pressure placed upon female international students who came from cultures that tend to view a woman's sole purpose of going to college to be finding a husband. Some of us also come from cultures in which arranged marriages are still common, and we struggle to talk about that in Western societies where such practice is generally viewed as oppressive, as opposed to our home societies where such practice is seen as valid. In the same study mentioned in the last chapter by Dr. Zachary S. Ritter, the results revealed a particular desire by heterosexual female participants to find prospective male partners with some level of exposure to Western family values, seeking to redefine their culture's traditional definitions of marriage and relinquish archaic patriarchal attitudes toward gender roles that are unfortunately still pervasive in most cultures around the world today.[38]

AMERICAN DATING 101

Different cultures also have very different interpretations of what the dating process entails. Unfortunately for me, it has resulted in a lot of miscommunication within my previous relationships, as well as on some dates with men. Globally, I think there is this sort of unspoken understanding if two people like each other, go on dates together, spend a lot of

---

38   Zachary S. Ritter, "Taboo or Tabula Rasa: Cross-Racial/Cultural Dating Preferences amongst Chinese, Japanese, and Korean International Students in an American University," *Journal of International Students*, Volume 5, Issue 4 (2015): 405-419.

time together, are always talking to each other, and do what are considered *"couple activities"* with one another (I'll leave that up to your imagination), then that's pretty much called "dating." However, in Western culture, you could be doing all of that and still not be considered "dating." It's not only that they're a lot more casual about it, there's also different steps necessary to progress from one stage to the next. So complicated is this aspect of American dating culture that the international student office at my university had to give us a presentation about this during our freshman orientation, but the best lesson, like all else in life, is always through firsthand experience.

In my first semester of sophomore year, I met this Mexican American dude through a friend. A few short conversations and one Halloween party later, and it was clear we were interested in each other. As a result, we were spending our weekends together, talked everyday together, went on dates where we shared food together, held hands together, and did, *you know, couple activities.* A few months had passed and, carelessly on my part, I had referred to myself as his "girlfriend," which resulted in us having to have that always slightly awkward conversation about "So, what are we?" He said we were "seeing each other." I didn't know what that really meant, so he ended up giving me a crash course on American dating right there in my living room.

When you go on those first few dates and are still in the process of getting to know each other, you're just "talking" to that person. The talking stage is "non-exclusive," meaning you can be talking to multiple people at once, which people in the West normally do. Once you have gotten to know the other person well enough and decide the both of you may possibly pursue something more long-term, you're "seeing" that person. The "seeing" stage can be both "non-exclusive" or "exclusive." Some people see multiple people at once, which means you two are "non-exclusively" seeing each other, and "it's not serious." Some people decide earlier on to invest their time and energy into just one person, which means you two are "exclusive" and "it's serious" because you're trying to see if you two can take the relationship to the next level. The next level is dating, which means you are their partner, but dating can be "exclusive" and "serious," or "non-exclusive" and is called an "open-relationship," which is likely "not serious" but it also could be "serious." The difference between the "talking" stage and the "seeing" stage are minimal at best because the lines between the two are *so fucking vague*, and it's these two initial dating stages where there is no verbal clarification or indication where the both of you stand with one another.

After becoming so accustomed to the American way of dating, coming back to Jakarta and adjusting myself to the local dating standards was like navigating a minefield. In countries like Indonesia, you pretty much just go from casual "talking" straight to serious "dating." Men here don't particularly appreciate it if I tell them I'm talking to other men besides them, even though we've only been talking for less than a week and it feels like a perfectly normal thing to do to me. The most shocking revelation I had was that parental involvement in a relationship begins as early as the talking stage. Many Indonesians—*apparently*—tend to have more traditional approaches of courting where they would not only have to take the time to meet their prospective partner's friends before deciding to pursue anything serious, but also their parents, siblings, grandparents, and any other extended family members who also need introducing. Once you've done all that and both parties' parents agree to the relationship, that officiates the dating status. This one dude I had only been talking to for less than two weeks was already talking about meeting my friends *and my mom,* after *the first date.* In American culture, people usually meet their non-married partner's parents only after they've started dating, and that's if they're even "seriously dating" as opposed to just "casual dating." In Indonesia, there is pretty much no such thing as "casual dating" because if you date at all, you are basically saying you intend to one day get married and have babies with that person, *and only that person.*

UNADULTERATED

In individualistic cultures like in the anglosphere, people have the discretion of selecting their own romantic partners, whether it be for dating or marriage. In collectivistic cultures, however, this process almost always has to involve the input of parents or other family members to ensure the prospective partner is a good fit within the family network. According to a study called "Dating and Mate Selection Among Young Adults from Immigrant Families," in the journal of *Marriage & Family Review,* results show while some variation is tolerable, most people from Hispanic, Latino, Asian, Arab, Eastern European, and African cultures traditionally have strong preferences for homogamous relationships in terms of ethnicity, religion, and culture.

However, this was less of a reflection of the participants' personal preferences and more of a reflection of their parents' preferences and expectations for them instead.[39] *Chi-*

---

39 Olena Nesteruk and Alexandra Gramescu, "Dating and Mate Selection Among Young Adults from Immigrant Families," *Marriage & Family Review,* Vol. 48, No. 1: 40-58.

nese Indonesian men aren't even my preference, they're my mother's! Outside of Chinese Indonesians, she'll make an exception for a few other Asian ethnicities, but that's pretty much it. Every time she talks about *me* finding a partner, it's always about what *she* wants and what *she's* looking for. At some point I get confused on who's the one dating and potentially marrying the guy—me or her? It's disheartening having to force myself to come to terms with the knowledge I could bring home any other man who checks all of my boxes, and yet no amount of integrity or the quality of his accomplishments may ever be enough to satisfy her.

Our parents' attitudes toward purposes of dating and marriage are also often very different to what most international students these days are more accustomed to believing in. Older generations, especially, have been hardened against the belief that love on its own is enough to get married, and therefore love isn't regarded as a priority. To them marriage is not so much about finding love as it is about attaining or elevating one's socioeconomic status, childbearing and expanding the family. Marriage in many other cultures is not about making you happy, it's about making your parents happy; it's not about what's best for you, but what's best for your family. Your own wedding isn't even for you and your partner, *it's for your parents and other relatives to enjoy and bask in the relief that you didn't end up as a fucking celibate.* Education, wealth, and compatibility to one's own culture, religion, language, and even *zodiac signs* were the defining factors of what made not a *perfect* and *happy* marriage, but an *economical* marriage. It is these differences in values between international students and our parents that can often make finding love and living at home extremely difficult.

* * *

Where independence and personal identity are highly stressed in individualistic cultures, unity and selflessness are stressed in collectivist cultures.[40] It is precisely this clash in orientation that results in people from both cultures having very different perceptions of adulthood. Adulthood in the Western definition often denotes pure, unadulterated free-dom—particularly from one's parents. Such concepts do not exist in non-Western cultures. Even as an "adult," which is defined differently in both cultures, you are still expected to consider and consult with your parents (or other members of the family) in whatever decision you make, even if it is for yourself. University or turning eighteen, which is normally when most Westerners start college, is often considered the right of passage into adulthood in the West. By the time they've graduated and gotten a job, they're expected to be completely self-reliant and live out on their own. That's not the case in most of the non-Western world. Being a gradu-ate, having a career, and even passing the age of twenty-one isn't enough to be considered an adult in many collectivist cultures. Often times, you're really only considered an actual adult once you're married. Even then, marriage in non-West-ern collectivist cultures does not entail anywhere near the same level of independence marriage in Western individu-alistic cultures do.

In Western cultures, it's not only normal for couples above the legal age to be living with one another, even prior to marriage, it's widely encouraged so couples can famil-iarize themselves with certain living habits and patterns of

40   "Understanding Collectivist Cultures," Kendra Cherry, March 24, 2020.

their partner so if they do end up getting married, they'll already be able to harmoniously live together. In Indonesia, it's normal for you to still live with your parents, or your partners' parents, *even after you're married*. It's even normal for additional family members like siblings, aunts, uncles, cousins, and even grandparents to live under the same roof. *I don't care what culture you are from, the thought of trying to make babies while your parents and other relatives are inside the house should be a universally scarring thought to anybody.*

In some cases, even after giving birth, it's still encouraged to continue living with your or your spouse's parents so they can be involved in taking care and raising the baby. *In terms of cost-efficiency and child safety however, it is admittedly a very effective alternative to hiring nannies or leaving them at daycare.* In other cases, married couples may move out (with or without children) but normally nowhere too far from either one of their parents. I have a friend who was allowed by his parents to finally move out with his wife under the condition they lived in the apartment building that's owned by his parents right across the street from their house. *When I'm married, my mom wants my husband to come live with us in our house.* It's something she low-key coerces me into doing in the name of "being a good daughter," but I guess at least she's not forcing it on me. So, I'm never going to have the experience of living alone with my boyfriend, but I *might* just be able to live alone with my husband one day.

All of this, especially within an intercultural context, begs the question, "Can my relationship survive all of this?" It's not even just a matter of if my future partner will be able to *understand*, but how much they actually will be able to *tolerate*. Consider the fact that even if I bring home someone of the same background who understands where all this is coming from, eliminating cultural difference won't necessarily eliminate generational difference. Amongst some of my Asian friends I've talked about this with, even *they* think my mom's requirements and expectations are a little too old-fashioned and extreme. In particular, it's especially the men who are unable to relate to having such stringent gender norms and restrictions *because let's not pretend that we don't still live in a world where boys are given much more freedom and independence compared to girls.*

THE LINE BETWEEN SELFISH AND SELFLESS

From a career standpoint, it's normal for people in collectivist societies to stay with their parents forever. *Heck, that's the expectation.* The concept of moving out of our parents' house to live by ourselves, or with friends once we've graduated and are working full-time jobs, is non-existent in most cultures. The pressure to go out and "be successful" is subverted to being closer with and taking care of family. Unfortunately, yet again this expectation is especially burdensome if you are a woman. Granted, I think this is mostly only applicable to those who actually have that kind of a luxury where they already have an established family business they can just immediately come home to. Undeniably, it is an immense amount of privilege to have, but acknowledging privilege does little to remedy the disappointing fact you never had that much of an option to forge a career path of your own the way you had wanted to.

The truth is I actually wanted to spend at least a few more years of my early twenties in Los Angeles. I wanted to work as an investment banker, have a nice apartment all to myself, make a five- or six-figure annual USD salary on my own and live the young, wild, sexy, and free life I've always dreamt of having. The bitter truth I've had to force myself to come to terms with is the fact I *did* have to give all of that up for my mother. My only consolation is it all happened in tandem with the coronavirus pandemic, so it felt like less of a situation I was forced into by a parent and more of the result of an unforeseeable tragedy beyond anyone's control.

The way I've always seen it is when many of my Western friends stay close to home, it's because they personally want to, but when many of my Asian friends and myself do, as bad as this might sound, it's more often than not out of cultural obligation. You are of course free to disagree with this, but in collectivist cultures, I don't think we see family as a *value.* To say something is a value means we *choose* to regard it as something that, *to ourselves,* deserves importance more than other things. Family, at least in most Asian cultures, was never made to be a choice, it's an obligation—a non-negotiable moral imperative. I think where the value lies is in whether or not we choose to commit to that obligation regardless of how we feel about it. It's not that we don't want to *ever* care and provide for our parents in their old age, but I think most of us wish we didn't have to commit to it so soon. I think it's especially the case when you are also the only child like me. I've always been a bit jealous of my friends who come from big families and have siblings because I feel like having one extra child in the family tends to loosen their parents' grip on them. The responsibility to take care of your parents or stay close to them is also not as heavy when you are sharing it amongst one or two other siblings. In my case, I have to be the only one to take care of my mom because there's no one else to do it. It's one of those things where it's not really a burden, but it's not really a choice either. I love my mom, and I want to be there for her, I just wish it didn't mean having to give up the other things I also wanted.

Collectivistic societies tend to focus so much on familial and communal togetherness it sometimes crosses the line into being smothering. To be completely and brutally honest, *that* is one of the reasons we wanted to go all the way to the anglosphere in the first place when we could've just gone to other countries and literally gotten more or less the same quality of education at a much cheaper price. Let's be honest here, more than just the prestige of being Western educated or the esteem of knowing you can afford to go to school there, deep down it's also because *most of us just want to get the fuck away from our parents.* Our parents aren't idiots, and deep down all of them know why we leave, it's just not something all of them are perhaps open about or even ready to admit to themselves.

Not only that, but many of us do whatever it takes to stay in our host countries after graduation, whether it's through getting a job that pays us a shitty salary, or working for a master's degree some of us don't even actually need. The only thing scarier than the possibility of the grass being less green on the other, non-Western side is the thought of having to move back home with our parents. *It's cheap, but at what cost?* We live with them for free at the expense of not only our autonomy, but also sometimes our emotional wellbeing and mental sanity. Moving abroad was the first time in many of our lives we finally had a taste of what it's like to just live life for ourselves instead of our parents. We got to be who we want to be instead of who they wanted us to be, and that's not an easy thing to suddenly have to give up and let go of. It's a hard pill to swallow that the realities once true for us back when we were still living in America,

Canada, Australia, or the UK no longer exists once we had to leave that life behind and move back to societies where those same values are not embraced.

BALANCING BOTH

Growing up, my mom always made it my job to keep her happy. She always asked, "Don't you want to see me happy?" as a way to get me to do whatever pleased her. Of course I want to make her happy, but is it so wrong for me to also have happiness separate from hers as well? Having grown up between one culture that is more selfish-oriented and another that is more selfless-oriented, I always had to figure out how to walk the fine line between both. Is it really selfish to think about myself and what I want first before I think about other people, even if it is my own parent? Is it wrong for us to have limitations on how much of ourselves, our freedom, and our dreams we are willing to sacrifice for our parents' sake? How much of myself can I selflessly give away to family or community before I reach the point where I no longer even exist on my own without them? In a time where the prioritization of one's own physical, mental, and emotional wellbeing is being embraced as a form of self-care, we have to wonder how much of that luxury is even available to people like us in the first place. While I'm still way too young to be thinking about having children (although some Asian aunties and uncles would look at me and vehemently disagree), writing all of this did force me to reflect on the kind of parent I want to be for my future children. How do I give them the best of both worlds I grew up with without compromising too much of one side for the other?

There's not a lot of choice in family, and it doesn't always feel fair, but beyond a shadow of a doubt, I know your patience will see you through to the other side. Our families really do just want the best for us, even if they might not always go about showing it the right way. I know that now that I'm a little older and wiser. I would like to believe that even the most stubborn of cultural rules which have been set in stone for generations hold no weight heavier than the love of our parents and their desire to simply see us happy and thrive. In truth, there isn't much consolation I am able to provide as someone who is still in the midst of trying to figure it all out for herself as well. I can only hope sharing my truth has brought—to those of you who could relate to this chapter—some reassurance in knowing you are not alone.

In the anglosphere, you are respected for the job you have, regardless of what it is. Every job has value, and subsequently, every human has value. If you clean bathrooms, pick up garbage, or bag groceries, it matters. You matter, and you get paid well for what those jobs are worth. In countries like India and UAE, those are considered third-class citizen jobs, and there's no respect for someone like that. I know if I went back to work as a journalist there, the financial and social value of my job would be nothing, but here in America, journalism counts for something. It is what keeps democracy in the light. When people say it's the land of opportunities, part of it means regardless of whatever job you have, you're going to be treated better (and paid better) than if you stayed back home doing the exact same thing.

—DAMITA MENEZES │ INDIA & UNITED ARAB EMIRATES

CHAPTER 10

THE REAL CULTURE SHOCK

BEYOND THE TV SCREEN

To me, sometimes it felt like people I met had the wrong idea of what sort of things I, as an international student, would experience culture shock about after coming to the States. I think some people tend to harbor this perception that life in other countries is otherworldly and different outside of developed Western nations. I was always unsure if it was because I was from Indonesia, or just the fact I was a foreigner in general. For many of us, coming to the anglosphere is really no different in terms of our access to basic services, like online shopping or amenities like Wi-Fi and electric cars, than if we were to remain back home or move to other countries. We wouldn't be shocked by the mundane aspects of living in a city. *It's not as if we came from rural villages with no access to technology and entertainment and have never lived in modern-day civilization.*

Over-exaggerated expectations of foreign countries aren't exclusive to people in the anglosphere, however. Whenever

I came back to Indonesia from the US, people were seldom direct in asking me what my life in the States was like because they had already adopted all of these hyper-glamorized misconceptions they grew up seeing on the media as conjectures of what real life in the States must be like.

It must be a lot more fun and exciting over there.

It's so nice that they have everything there.

Why would you come back here?

Isn't it better to live there?

In reality, my life in America was different, but it wasn't overall any better or worse than my life in Indonesia. It also just depends on *where* in the United States you are, just as it depends on *where* you are in Canada, Australia, and the United Kingdom. The entire anglosphere is not a gigantic concrete metropolis like New York, Toronto, London, and Sydney. Los Angeles is a very fun city with endless activities to do, places to explore, and attractions galore *if you have the money to indulge in those things.* True to its glamorous Hollywood reputation, it has some of the most physically attractive people I've ever seen, which has definitely done some damage to my self-esteem—but that's beside the point. Otherwise, in my opinion, it's actually not too different from Jakarta. They both have horrible traffic, everybody has to have a car because public transportation is shit, there are beggars on every street, the population is huge, and drinking tap water will give you diarrhea.

Perhaps the most eerie resemblance between the two, however, is their urban inequality—an intriguingly beautiful but also disastrous amalgam of the spatial and social division between the modern rich and the urban poor. The Shangri-La Hotel in Jakarta is located right behind a slum. A three-minute drive from my upscale Silicon Beach neighborhood will take me to a low-income neighborhood where poverty, drugs, and crime are rampant. This was probably one of the more shocking revelations I had after moving to the US, traveling to different states, and seeing the country *not* through a television screen. There are so many parts of America and Los Angeles that are still incredibly impoverished and underdeveloped, and when I explain that to friends and other people who've never seen that side of LA or America before, they're always so shocked. Other international friends who go to school in Canada, Australia, or the UK have also commented the exact same thing—how it's not as glitzed and glammed up as other people had expected it to be. For the longest time, the world has always accepted this false image of anglosphere countries as these utopias, this fantasy of them being these technologically advanced and highly industrialized places with profound economic prosperity and robust infrastructure, while the rest of the world is limping behind them. In reality, these countries struggle just as much as the rest of us.

THE CULTURE OF HARD WORK

And with those struggles come a cultural value so central to the American and Canadian identity, it has created the very fabric of their society as we know it today—hard work. The truth is my biggest culture shock of coming to the US was seeing how much harder life actually was there. Of course, it's especially shocking for kids like me who come from more sheltered lives back home, but regardless, I think there is a general consensus amongst those of us who have experienced living in North America that life there tends to be a lot more stressful and overwhelming. It's not to say life in other countries like Indonesia (or even in the UK and Australia who, I've been told, are not so big on the whole "hustle culture") is necessarily "easier," but I think it's much *simpler* in comparison, especially compared to the US.

The US is incredibly career-conscious and individualistic to a fault. LA's nice, but she's certainly not the most forgiving. It's everyone for themselves in a city too big, too busy, and too competitive to give a shit about how you feel. In America, there is a serious cultural expectation to always be doing the most. You have to be the most driven, the most ambitious, the busiest, the strongest, the boldest, and the most accomplished. Almost all my American friends have had to get their first jobs by fifteen and get their driver's license and drive themselves everywhere by sixteen. Most were expected to move out of their parents' home by the time they're nineteen and in college, and they had to be completely financially independent by the time they were twenty-two and graduated, with a well-paying, full-time job secured even before getting their hands on their degrees. That's why most of them worked one, if not multiple, part-time jobs and/or an internship. I even knew kids who studied *and worked* full-time, on top of juggling college, to help them pay off their student loans and support living expenses like rent, gas, and food *almost entirely by themselves.*

I'm twenty-four and still don't have my driver's license. In Jakarta, I have a driver who drives me around *in my mom's car*—and that's nothing out of the ordinary. Many households in Jakarta have personal drivers who work for them around the clock, and some companies even assist their expat workers in finding a personal chauffeur. I never got my first job until I was twenty years old in college, now *that* is considered out of the ordinary where I'm from. Most Indonesian kids don't get their first paid positions until after they have completed university, and the idea of working anything beyond a summer internship while still a student is unheard of. In the anglosphere, when you're a student, you're also expected to be an adult, but when you're a student in other cultures in the rest of the world, *you're just a student.* You're supposed to just study hard, get good grades, do whatever it takes to graduate at the top of your class, and then get the fuck out of there. For international students, in the eyes of both our families and the law, that is our only purpose of coming to the anglosphere.

For the international students who already come from well-off families—or at least families that are financially secure enough where we have the option to either evade, or grow with, societal pressures—we have more space to prioritize our studies and take on fun leisure activities on the side like arts and sports to fill up our schedules. We can focus on finding jobs and internships that deliver a more fruitful experience, even if it means getting paid a lesser rate or not getting paid at all. That's if we even want to do all that in the first place, because we don't need those experiences to go back home and take over the family business. However, not all of us are like that. Many of the international students coming to the anglosphere come from backgrounds where they don't have the financial security to escape societal marginalization or political instability back in their home countries. They are the ones fighting tooth and nail to stay in the anglosphere after college because they don't have much of a future to return to back home.

HONORING THE STRUGGLE

In America, people praise and admire my single mom for how strong and resilient she is. Despite all of the obstacles that came with having to chase after a career and raise a child all by herself, she persevered and excelled at both beyond flying colors. They understand it's a difficult position to be in, and they honor that struggle. I was always encouraged to embrace her story and be proud of the life she and I have lived. In Indonesia, most people just choose to look down on the fact that marriage was just never something she wanted, neither before nor after having me. Being a single mother was—and for the most part still is—considered dishonorable. It's a shame that would not only define her for the rest of her life but would also be passed down for me to inherit for the rest of mine. Back in high school, there was a Chinese Indonesian boy in my year who told one of the new students in my grade to steer clear from me because I was "the daughter of an unmarried woman." I grew up having kids and adults put me down for being raised without a dad. Coming from a broken home was always their explanation for what they saw as my weaknesses and shortcomings, but my only saving grace has always been the fact *I at least come from money.* It's the one thing I have that, in other people's eyes, forgives me and my mom of our unfortunate familial background, and it's the only reason that despite being a woman, an ethnic minority, and a religious minority, I can still come back to Indonesia and have a future. In another life, if I were to still be born into the same situation without any of the financial privileges I have now, I honestly don't think there would be any hope of me ever climbing up that social and corporate ladder.

In America, people value hard work and the exhaustive strive required to earn every single dollar that's theirs and theirs alone. You could be a janitor, a courier worker, a construction worker, a dishwasher, *or even a single mom*, and as long as you can show you are working hard toward a personal goal to better your life and the lives of those you love, people will respect you. Even if you fail, as long as you try and give it your best shot, that's all that matters. Your ability to work hard is the *one* defining thing that warrants other people's respect for you as an individual, but in many other cultures, that hustle mentality is just considered an optional asset to have in a person. The way I could earn respect from Americans was to show them, above all else, I was a hard worker just like them. I knew how to be independent, pull my own weight, and stand on my own two feet. Often times, I felt like the only way I could earn respect from most of the Indonesian international students was if I showed them, above all else, I come from a family that could afford the exact same things they did, such as: eating out at expensive restaurants every other night, driving a fancy car, wearing designer fashion and owning designer products, buying $1000 VIP tickets to Coachella, celebrating my birthdays at nightclubs that cost $2,000–3,000 per table *with* bottle service, and own a $4000 Cartier bracelet.

In individualistic societies, indulging in such luxuries would still be more respectable if it was achieved by the merit of one's own labor and not something afforded to them as a result of their parents' hard work. In other cultures, there is no distinction between the two. Like the money, the respect is something—to them—they inherited, not something they were ever taught to have to work for and earn. In a way, I think this is the disconnect with some international students whenever they show up to class wearing Gucci or pull up to campus in a Lamborghini. Sometimes it might not even come from a shallow place of wanting to show off how rich they are, although sometimes it definitely does. It's just that the idea that one should work for what they have in order to deserve it, or be respected for having it in the first place, is not a cultural value that registers where they are from, especially not in Indonesia. Especially for those coming from more financially privileged positions—whether that means having just enough to live comfortably in one lifetime or having enough to last the lifetime of two or three future generations—there is this expectation from other people (sometimes even our own parents) that we would *just do the bare minimum*. It's not even necessarily because most of us are *so filthy rich we can just never work a day in our lives* (although some undoubtedly are), it's just that unless there is a *genuine and urgent need* to work *that* hard, many of us just won't. There isn't a lot of incentive to challenge and push your own limits, and in true collectivistic fashion, the idea of becoming somebody of your own, *on your own,* does not really exist either.

One could argue it's less to do with a difference in culture, but rather more to do with a difference in social class. Granted, the majority of my American circles tend to fall within the upper-lower-class to the lower-middle-class range, whereas the majority of my international circles tend to fall within the upper-middle-class to *their-nation's-top-1-percent* range. I would argue, however, it is actually an intersection of both. Some of my wealthier American friends who afford more lavish and relaxed lifestyles still value finding employment during college and having the ability to financially and physically support themselves, even if only by a little. One of the most admirable things I've learned about Americans is even when offered the chance to not work as hard, many of them still won't take you up on that offer and, to me, *this* was the real culture shock of coming to America. Yes, life there is much harder, much more intense and much more unforgiving, but that's why Americans are some of the hardest working people in the world, ***and god damn are they proud of that.***

* * *

In cultures like Indonesia, people only honor status and results; there's no value to how you get there, just as long as you do. There's such a high expectation to not only be as perfect as possible, but to also achieve perfection as effortlessly as possible. You and your family have to fall within a certain income bracket, work certain roles within particular professions, afford lavish lifestyles, *but make it look easy, like you just shat all of that out of your ass overnight,* just to have people even look at you with some dignity and respect. Hardships are not something to be proud of overcoming. They're something to be ashamed of having in the first place. You could be the most diligent and ambitious person in the room, even the most well-connected, but it holds no weight against those whose families have more money than you. It's not admirable to work hard; it's admirable to have been born not having to work hard, or even cheating yourself into an easier life through corruption or marrying rich.

At least back in LA, people never cared about who I was, where I came from, or what I could or could not afford—just what I have done and can do. People work hard and encourage others to work harder, too, because despite various socioeconomic and political forces making it difficult, it's the American ideology if *everybody* takes responsibility of their own lives and stays persistent, they will be rewarded for their endeavors one day. This ideology exists in the rest of the anglosphere as well. America may not be the greatest country in the world, and neither are Canada, Australia, or the UK, but nobody can deny they are great countries, and *this* is why. These nations are great not just because they have the legal liberty to pursue personal goals and the economic opportunities to compete for success, but because their people also genuinely believe those freedoms are made for *everyone,* regardless of social status, gender, age, race, culture, or religion. Sadly, in a lot of other countries, people don't have enough faith in that idea. In a lot of countries, people don't believe you could have been a single mom living on government benefits and then become the world's first billionaire author (J.K Rowling), or that you could have worked as a PE teacher and then become one of Hollywood's highest paid actors (Hugh Jackman). [41,42] They don't see how you could have gone from living paycheck to paycheck to becoming the most streamed artist of the decade (Drake), or how you could have been scooping ice cream at a Baskin Robbin's and then one day become the 44th President of the United States (Barack Obama).[43,44] This concept of working hard and being able to change your life so drastically just does not exist where many of us are from.

Where I'm from, it's not the norm for people to dream of the moon, stars, and rainbows unless they're rich and powerful enough to afford such aspirations. Most people

41 Leslie Albrecht, "Harry Potter at 20: How J.K. Rowling went from welfare to billion-dollar wizards," *MarketWatch,* June 27, 2017

42 Emmy Potter, "How Hugh Jackman Went From Teaching PE To Wolverine," *Looper,* April 21, 2017.

43 Omar Sanchez, "Drake is Spotify's most-streamed artist of the decade," *EntertainmentWeekly,* December 3, 2019.

44 Chris D'Angelo, "How Obama's 'Brutal' First Job Inspired A New Youth Employment Initiative," *HuffPost,* Updated December 19, 2016.

settle with what they were born into, even if what they were born into isn't even that great, because most people believe they should just stay in their lanes. They would rather not try than fail and lose face in front of everybody they know. Many years ago, I had a maid who was telling me about her kids back in the village, all of whom were below the age of twenty-five and were already carrying on the family tradition of working as domestic helpers. I asked her if her kids ever had other ambitions besides becoming maids and drivers. She responded, "People from small backgrounds like us, we can't dream too big. I wouldn't encourage them even if they did. This is our fate by God, we should just accept that. What matters is we find a halal way of living so when He calls us, we're allowed into heaven. Besides, to become a doctor? A lawyer? A businessman? It's not in our place." I couldn't help but wonder if in another life, in an alternate reality where things were different and maybe they had the opportunity to move to a country like the US, UK, Canada, or Australia, her kids could've grown up doing much bigger things in life than just driving trucks and scrubbing toilets.

SELF-MADE PERSON

It's not a bad thing to be content with one's life as is, or to want the "simple life" (however way you choose to define that). Most people in general do and that's fine, but you have kids like me who *don't* want to settle for the "simple life." There are kids like me who *do* want to reach for the moon, stars, and the rainbows, but are constantly told our dreams are too big in a society too small to see the point in any of it. When I think about it, I think this is one of the most honest reasons, deep down, why so many of us grew up so attracted to the idea of living in the anglosphere, whether it be for a few years of college or forever after that. Beyond the prestige (or even the distance to get away from our parents), we go there for a shot at being "self-made." We want to make something of ourselves and be defined by the things we can hold ourselves accountable for rather than the circumstances we were forcibly born into – no matter how bad or how good those are. We want our hard work valued for its worth, and that eventually there is a reward to reap somewhere down the line for it. The whole idea of being an entirely "self-made person" exists everywhere around the world, but it's an idea that is valued more in individualistic societies like the anglosphere.

For some of us, we go there because it's a place where no dream is considered too big. You could be a maid, a truck driver, a regular working-class person, or a refugee, and have a shot at either making a better living doing the same thing you were doing back home or becoming something more than that. For others who are more privileged, like me, we go there because we don't just want to dream big, we want to dream bigger, because in truth that ability to dream larger than life itself comes from a place of immense privilege most people back home do not have. The fruits of our parents' (and/ or grandparents') labor have been collected into an assorted basket of ripened opportunities we've always been able to feast upon since birth, and it's created this ambition of not only wanting to see who we are *without it*, but what we can do *with it*. How much of the wealth, power, and privilege we hold was acquired by us, instead of associated to us? How much of what we have and what we've built is the result of our own merit, and not of those who came before us? How do we use our privilege for a good that's greater than just our own, so we can prove the value of the culmination of everything that's always been given to us?

FINAL STRETCH

I came to the US thinking I could find more opportunity than any other place could offer a small island, Filipino girl like me. It's a very sobering experience to realize all of that is just a facade as soon as you get here. It's a lot to feel for somebody still so young, to know you are reduced to a piece of paperwork that is going to be immediately put into the recycling bin of every HR or audition room, and that no quality of work, strength of character, or any amount of integrity will help you.

—NATASHA AQUINO | PHILIPPINES & SRI LANKA

CHAPTER 11

"SORRY, WE DON'T SPONSOR INTERNATIONAL STUDENTS"

AGAINST ALL ODDS

During my junior year of college, I worked part time at my university's career center as a peer advisor where I helped other LMU students and alums with resumes, cover letters, networking strategies, how to go about finding a job or internship, and other career and professional development related services & advice. At the time, I was one of three international students on the team who, on top of handling the domestic students with regular inquiries, were also sometimes the point of contact for the international students coming in to ask about how to file for specific work authorizations, get a social security number, and all of the cruel and unforgiving truths that come with trying to get hired while on a student visa.

One morning while on shift, a Burmese international student came to the office asking to see a peer advisor and was paired up with me. I was shocked to find out she was only a freshman in her second semester but was already stressing out over having the right resume and applying for jobs. She had her eyes set on applying for this waitressing job at a family-owned restaurant hiring not too far from campus, and she said they'd pay her well. There was just one problem with that. First year international students in the United States are not allowed to work off-campus. I told her while she does have the option of applying for an on-campus job, most of those only hire students with Federal Work-Study, which provides part-time campus jobs for *domestic* undergraduate and graduate students *on financial aid*. The disappointment on her face was clear, and she was disheartened by the harsh reality of how much more difficult it was going to be for her to help her parents fund the extortionate costs of living in Los Angeles, at least for that first year.

Applying for jobs and internships was the absolute *bane of my fucking existence*. Across all four years, I had applied to over a hundred part time jobs, including internships and other forms of paid work on and off campus in the US, and was only ever hired three times in total. There were only around ten offices at my university that accepted international student workers when I was applying toward the end of my sophomore year, and all of them—with the exception of one—had rejected me. *Sorry, we don't sponsor international students* was the soundtrack playing in the backdrop of every recruitment event I went to and stamped on every job application I submitted online. Most of the time I was never even selected for interviews, and the few times I have been lucky enough to be selected, I would often never hear back from them past the second round after being asked *"Do you require sponsorship now or in the future?"* By the time I would be done explaining the process to them, they would have already made up their minds not to hire me anyway.

From the career coaching side of universities, by far the two hardest populations to help in a profound way are the international students and students with really severe disabilities because the job market in the US is incredibly biased against both of them.

—KYLE KIM-GREENBERG | UNITED STATES OF AMERICA (ALSO MY FORMER BOSS)

What is the work authorization process in the US like for international students? The only hefty process is the optional practical training (OPT) application, which usually starts at the beginning of our final semester before graduating. *I promise I won't bore you with all the formal legal bullshit. Just hear me out, and you'll understand exactly why this shit's such a pain in the ass.* Applying for an OPT is one thing. Going through the immigration process is **another thing**. The very basic process of applying for an OPT is after you apply, you wait for a card to arrive in the mail. If before you got the card you were lucky enough to have been offered a job, you need to wait until that card has arrived to be allowed to start working and get paid for that work legally.

If you still don't have a job offer after you have received the card, you have ninety days (three months) to find a job, otherwise you need to leave the country. Ideally, you find an employer that hires you within (or before) those ninety days and then agrees to sponsor you for your work visa once those ninety days are up. We need to be sponsored to be eligible to even enter the immigration process to acquire a work visa in the first place. On top of that, the process of getting an H-1B work visa is done through entering a *fucking lottery. Did you know that apparently there's a 45 percent chance of any author to write a New York Times Bestseller?*[45] *That's higher than the 32 percent odds of me getting selected for a work visa in America during the 2019–2020 season.*[46]

The problem most of us run into is most companies and employers *don't want to sponsor international students*, so getting hired at all was already a bigger challenge than average—even for internships. There are technically no additional legal procedures for companies to hire us as interns, but most companies want to hire interns who have the potential to be offered a full-time position with them after graduation and extending a full-time offer would eventually require them to sponsor a work visa. **Even if they do decide to sponsor us, it doesn't guarantee we'll get the visa.** I know people who got jobs at companies willing to sponsor them after graduation, but when they entered the visa lottery, their application didn't get selected, so they had to leave the US and either quit that job or work remotely for them from some other country. *So even if companies hire you and were willing to invest the time (and maybe even money) to sponsor your visa, just because*

45 Jacob Shelton, "Crazy Odds That Will Surprise You," *Ranker,* Accessed February 26, 2021.

46 "H-1B Lottery 2019-2020 | Results, Process, and Chances (Updated 4/12/19)," *SGM Law Group,* Publication April 12, 2019.

they want to keep you around doesn't mean the government does. Most of my international friends from my graduating class, or the class one year prior, applied for OPT and applied for jobs within the ninety days, and a majority of them never got hired in time before they had to pack up and leave.

Every single time I would apply for a very nice company I wanted to work for, and I knew I was perfectly qualified and would crush the job, the position would always go to the American, and I knew between the two of us it came down to the very last interview stage. Their explanation was always just, "To be honest, we would pick you, but we just can't sponsor you." It just becomes difficult and extremely discouraging to follow through with what we want in our careers and our lives, which is to chase after a better standard of living and quality of life. In the end, I ended up moving to Canada, hoping I can stay here for good, find a better job, and find a better life.

—BENEDICT LEO RAHADJA | INDONESIA

BRICK WALLS

According to the US Department of State, the total number of international students enrolled in the US in the 2019–2020 academic year was 1,075,496, making up 5.5 percent of the total US student body. Out of that total number, 223,539 were those who had graduated and were in the process of filing for OPT—the highest number of international students to ever seek full-time employment post-graduation in the last ten years.[47] Yet, many US employers still do not understand

---

47   "Enrollment Trends: International Student Data From The 2020 *Open Doors® Report." Open Doors®*, Accessed February 26, 2021.

what the process of sponsoring international students really entails. Majority of the responsibility falls upon us to hire and directly communicate with an immigration attorney to prepare the paperwork, and many students even take it upon themselves to pay all the processing fees—not the companies hiring them. Regardless, because of this lack of awareness, it's always easier for them to reject our applications. It's a combination of being both unbothered and intimidated by an immigration system they knew was just as complicated as it was cut-throat.

Over more recent years there has been a shift in where international students are choosing to pursue higher education, with Canada and Australia seeing rapid increases, while the US and the UK are seeing falling or stagnating numbers—unsurprising as to why. In Canada, as long as you have studied there, all you have to do is apply for the Post-Graduation Work Permit Program (PGWPP) after graduation. It's based on the length of your degree program. If your degree program was more than two years long, you get three years afterwards to work. If your degree was anywhere between eight months and less than two years, then the work permit will be the same length as your degree program.[48] In Australia, as long as you have studied there for at least two years, you have six months following your graduation date to apply for a 485 Temporary Graduate visa (Post-Study Work Stream), which gives you anywhere between two to four years to work (depending on qualifications).[49] This is why I don't talk about Canada and Australia a lot in this chapter;

---

48 "Post-Graduation Work Permit Program (PGWPP)," Government of Canada, Accessed February 26, 2021.

49 "Temporary Graduate visa (subclass 485) Post-Study Work Stream," *Australian Government Department of Home Affairs,* Accessed February 26, 2021.

there's really no need *to because they have it so much easier than those of us based in the US or the UK.*

Student visa data shows the number of international students at US universities declined by 2.2 percent at the undergraduate level and 5.5 percent at the graduate level from fall 2016 to 2017 after years of substantial growth. The decline was attributed to a range of factors including reductions in scholarship programs sponsored by foreign governments, issues of cost and affordability, uncertainty about visa policies, the future availability of post-study work opportunities, and concerns about physical safety. *Not to mention, a certain presidential administration had painted the US as a less welcoming place to foreign nationals.*[50] Simon Marginson, director of the Centre for Global Higher Education at University College London, published an article in 2018 where he projected Australia would soon overtake the UK as the second-largest global destination for international students.[51] He was right.

Back in October of 2019, I heard about upcoming legislation that would allow international students on the Tier 4 visa an extra two years after graduation to secure employment. My timing was unfortunate. I had graduated a few months earlier in July and, according to the legislation at the time, my visa was set to expire at the end of the month. To switch from a student visa to a work visa, you need a minimum annual salary between £20,800 and £30,000 (depending on the occupation).

50 Elizabeth Redden, "International Student Numbers Decline," *Inside Higher Ed,* Publication January 22, 2018.

51 Simon Marginson, "The UK in the global student market: second place for how much longer?" *Centre For Global Higher Education,* Published July 19, 2018.

Journalism is an industry, at least in London, where workers are more in supply than demand. Everyone wanted someone with years of experience for a supposedly "entry-level" job, and the salary rarely met the bottom end of the requirement for the visa. My only other option was to do an unpaid internship for a year just so I could extend my stay with a Tier 5 intern visa and stay in the country long enough to find another job. But why should I have to go a year without pay, without people valuing my time and work, just because the nationality on my passport is wrong?

—CLAIRE JISOO CHUNG | UNITED STATES, SOUTH
KOREA, INDONESIA, & UNITED KINGDOM

As of 2020, Australia hosts 664,000 international students, while the UK hosts only 485,000 students, falling behind Canada who hosts 642,000 students. [52,53,54] This comes as no surprise considering how the UK scaled back its post-study work options in 2011, around the same time Australia expanded their opportunities for international students to stay and work post-grad. Not to mention various other migration policies and Home Office regulations which have also contributed to making the UK an increasingly unattractive place for international students.[55]

---

52   "Education Data: Monthly Summary of International Student data (YTD November 2020)," *Australian Government, Trade and Investment Commission,* Accessed February 26, 2021.

53   "International Student Statistics in UK 2020," *Study in UK,* Accessed February 26, 2021.

54   Kareem El-Assal, "642,000 international students: Canada now ranks 3rd globally in foreign student attraction," *CIC News,* Published on February 20th, 2020

55   Ibid. 53

And because most of us *chose* to come all the way here to pursue our educations and careers, somehow it means we're "asking for it." *If it's so hard for you to get a job here, then why don't you just move back to your own country? If you don't like it here, then leave.* International students are also often at the receiving end of racist and xenophobic anti-immigration vitriol, and it either goes unnoticed because nobody gives a shit, or unreported because most international students either don't want to or are too scared to speak up about it. If the people saying these things were the same people who came from countries like Indonesia, where the salary range for *all* entry level employees is anywhere between US\$350–700 **per month**, *they wouldn't want to go back either.* The only job offer I got in Jakarta after graduation (which, by the way, ended up rejecting me *after* I had accepted my offer) offered me a \$565 monthly salary. It doesn't matter I was educated abroad; the job market in my home country doesn't give importance to my foreign credentials in terms of pay or starting position.

Unfortunately, most of the international students are highly skilled and usually really hard-working but still can't find jobs. No one looks at your hard work when it comes to the end of your studies. I have seen a lot of first-class honors students from the likes of LSE, Imperial, UCL, and all of these top schools who spent more than £70,000 on their education, doing £250-per-month jobs in Delhi, India.

—SHIVAM CHAUHAN | INDIA

Not all of us are coming home to rich families with already-established family businesses we can just take over. Not all of us can just sit back and enjoy all the wealth and luxury that has been handed to us by our parents or grandparents. Even for those of us who come from more financially stable families, that doesn't mean we don't have to worry about how we are going to sustain ourselves and our families after graduation. We give up being with family and other people we love to chase after higher salaries and better qualities of life few other countries outside of the Western developed world can provide *because that's exactly what we've always been told.* For centuries, the US and the UK have always touted themselves as *the* best countries in the world; they're the golden lands with opportunities aplenty for anybody and everybody who wish to strive for greatness and success. When we do end up taking their word on that promise of a better life, we're suddenly hit with the realization those opportunities have never been made with people like us in mind.

I think the most common assumption is international students hail from wealthy familial backgrounds. While it is true for many of us, it is an immense privilege to study in English in our own home country, many families like mine are not making millions, and tuition is definitely a financial strain. Whenever there is conversation about financial aid, I always feel slightly uncomfortable because I have a friend whose family has higher earnings than mine that received financial aid all because she holds a local passport, while I am denied financial aid of any kind for the next three years. At the same time, I feel I would be judged harshly by being honest about the fact I'm paying full tuition.

—ANONYMOUS | CHINA

Point is, it just sucks. We're always the ones having to pay tuition fees that are significantly higher than domestic students, and yet we're the ones never eligible for most scholarships or other forms of financial aid. We often work the lowest-paying jobs on campus as well. We are made to deliver stellar academic results and have impeccable resumes, while dealing with massive brick walls of immigration laws and government legislations which do *everything* to make sure we get out of the country as soon as possible. We're at the mercy of immigration systems uninterested in looking out for neither our present or future well-beings, and nobody—not even our parents, sometimes—ever stop to consider what that level of stress and anxiety on a daily basis can do to a person. None of us are expecting special treatment to get hired. We just want to be given a fair shot to even compete in the first place.

At my university, if first-year international students wanted to get a job, we didn't have the option of choosing where we wanted to work on campus. Instead, we all had to start out as dishwashers and cooking assistants at the school cafeteria. We filed a complaint to the school because many of us honestly thought it was quite racist and xenophobic of them. It was unfair the domestic students had the liberty of working at any campus office they wanted, and not only were we not given that choice, but we were also placed at the bottom of the job pyramid.

—SALOMÉ VALDIVIESO | ECUADOR

TO BE GIVEN A CHANCE

A few years ago, I had a professor named Tony Kmetty. Particularly, I remember how he dedicated a few minutes of his lecture to explain what the job-recruiting process for international students—specifically—entailed and the struggles and challenges that came with it. He talked about how the odds are always stacked against us, and that it isn't always a fair fight. He turned to the domestic students in that class and said something along these lines: one day, they are going to become the future leaders of America, and it was important that they knew all of this information so that one day they are in a position to help the future generation of international students, that many moons ago could have been some of us international students sitting there in that classroom with them at that very moment.

He was the only professor I've had throughout all my four years who I can remember ever acknowledging international students in front of an entire class—let alone within the context of career and employment, which is where we're normally met with apathy from domestic students under the impression that we're too privileged to be deserving of their pity. One of the domestic students raised their hand to ask a follow-up question, and I couldn't help but think that perhaps for many of the other domestic students in that room, this was their first time hearing and learning about this issue.

Although this book is mostly targeted towards international students and third-culture kids, in many ways I've tried to make it accessible to people outside of those groups as well—at the very least being domestic students from the anglosphere who've picked up this book either out of pure curiosity on the international perspective, or support and solidarity with the internationals they have in their lives. If any Americans, Brits, Canadians and Australians are reading this, I hope one day when you are the ones sitting at those corporate desks making recruitment decisions that have the power to alter the course of one's entire livelihood, that Professor Kmetty's message to my class resonates with you the way it did with that one student.

I hope you'd look at all of the international student applicants and see that we are worthy of being given a chance; that we shouldn't have to beg for the chance to stay in a country that has always said it wants talent, intellect, and hard work, but for some reason not when it's coming from people like us. As international students we can work with you to put a call to action, but ultimately the voices with the privilege of citizenship will always be more impactful than ours, and the only thing that we can ask of you is to stand up and demand universities and companies to do more. Demand businesses to invest more in the international bodies they want to profit from. Demand more from governments that are oppressing international students, and fight for our rights too. People will say there's nothing that can be done. Once upon a time not so long ago, I gave in to the exact same narrative myself, but I have seen how when one voice is joined by the chorus of many, it can move mountains and bring us one step closer to making a change, and just maybe, this book could be a start.

FACING REALITY

The harsh reality is that many of us do end up forced to leave our host countries, and there's nothing anybody or anything outside the power of politicians, or the good grace of some higher being, can do about it when it happens. The question is, where do you have left to go from here? What do you do when the rug has been pulled from underneath your feet, and you are left to feel like every chance you've ever had for that *bright and shiny future* has suddenly been taken away from you? It's a hard reality to come face to face with, knowing you could have given it your all—applied to all the jobs available, messaged and followed up with every recruiter you met at every networking event you attended, milked the shit out of all the resources provided to you on campus, took in every single career tip and piece of advice you've ever been given—and it would still never be enough. You could have been the perfect candidate, and it would still hold no weight against the burden of your foreignness. You'd still run out of time. You'd still be sent home. You'd still have spent hundreds of thousands of dollars on an education that provided little to no return on your investment, or at least not in the way you'd hoped it would. You could have gone down on your knees and prayed for a miracle, and neither god nor the universe would still be in your favor.

The only thing you can do is force yourself to trust that there is a much bigger world out there. Repeat to yourself in the mirror you didn't let anybody down, because the truth is you really didn't. It is a loss, but it isn't entirely yours to bear, because the patch of earth you've been standing on also loses you, and all of the valuable skills, insights, stories, and perspectives that could have made it greener. Accept the fact *perhaps it is just part of the universe's plan to fuck you up the ass with a sledgehammer once in a while* in hopes it forces you individually, and subsequently humanity collectively, to gauge progress, evolve, and continue moving forward. The human mind will always choose to dwell on the negative feelings that occur after an inevitable event with unfavorable outcomes have occurred but know that pain and suffering are not everlasting. Not necessarily the metaphor "time heals all wounds," but rather it is what we do with that time that heals. The human brain, in the midst of pain and suffering, will constantly search for ways to combat agony and sorrow, because that is what we're fundamentally created for. If anything, history has proven time and time again that even in the face of unfathomable tragedy and great loss, we always rise above the occasion and continue to be okay. It is the human condition that we always seek survival, and it is perhaps the universal condition that we always find it.

The notion the US is "the land of opportunities" is so exagger-
ated—not false, just exaggerated. That phrase makes it seem
as if the moment you step foot into the US, there are going to
be ribbons, rallies, and so many job opportunities waiting for
you, only for you to then come here and realize not all of them
are always going to be for you. I've had to learn that fact in
my own time. They don't tell you all about the expenses that
are required, the connections you never knew you needed, the
racism that is very much still there, nor the ridiculous pedestal
capitalism is held on. Not trying to be so negative—I've had
the opportunity to do things I otherwise would not have been
able to do in my home country as a film major. I just wish I
was less naive at the beginning of this journey.

—MICHELLE KAMUNYO | KENYA

In the West, I think there is more support and acceptance—
both formal and casual—for someone who wants to make it
on their own. There is also infrastructure and laws for guid-
ance. I agree there are many opportunities there, in general,
but unless you are a citizen or permanent resident, accessing
those resources may be close to impossible.

—ANONYMOUS | UNITED STATES, AUSTRALIA,
UNITED KINGDOM, MALAYSIA, SINGAPORE,
INDONESIA, & THAILAND

From the perspective of an American being an international
student in Europe: A lot of my American friends want to work
in France or other parts of Europe after graduation, but they
don't have the European passport that can allow them to
legally stay there after their studies. It makes me sad because

they really are some of the smartest and most talented kids I know, and they're getting passed up for jobs they'd otherwise get back home, no problem. For international students in Europe, it's not the financial burden of sponsoring you, it's just the paperwork burden—recruiters and companies here just don't want to deal with all that. If there's any takeaway from me saying this, it is that it's not super easy on the other side either guys, I promise.

—JENNA GALOWICH | UNITED STATES & FRANCE

I majored in civil engineering and most companies were not willing to sponsor us for H1-B visas. I used to not mention I would need sponsorship down the road, just so it wouldn't jeopardize my options of getting hired. Later on, I realized I was just wasting my time, and the companies' times too, by not disclosing this information before being invited to the interviews. There comes a point where I'd have to tell them "hey, by the way, I can work under OPT for the first year, and possibly extend it for an additional seventeen months, but will require H1-B sponsorship after that," and immediately the response would be "Oh unfortunately, we don't/can't do that, but we appreciate you coming to the interview."

—GALO EMILIO BOWEN | ECUADOR

It's not enough that you're better, or the best, you need to be the best of the best. You always have to go one step beyond everyone else. If I were studying back in Japan, I think completing undergraduate school would have been enough to get me a pretty good job there, but I was so adamant about working here in London, and I realized a bachelor's degree wasn't going to cut it. I ended up having to make that big time and financial commitment to get a master's.

—MIKA SUZUKI | JAPAN, UNITED KINGDOM, & INDONESIA

Most bigger companies have a training period that lasts up to a year, and averages around 9 months from my experience. I have a Masters in Finance from the Johns Hopkins University, but that didn't even really matter, because the training period would basically eat up all my OPT time. No company wants to hire someone, train them for 1 year, and then have them go work for another company. Or, have to sponsor them before even knowing your work performance.

—PETER NUARI YUWONO | INDONESIA

When I finally heard back from one of the companies I applied to that I was hired for my first internship, I just started sobbing. As an international student, my tears were more than just for joy of knowing my hard work had paid off. For me, it was like coming up for a breath of fresh air and realizing that the uncertainty brought on by immigration may just start to settle and find some balance. It was a sliver of a break from constantly feeling like the rug was going to be pulled out from under me at any second. One thing I urge international students to do is to never give up on themselves. It will be hard, you may cry, but you'll also have some great moments. It's all part of the journey that tells your complete story - enjoy it! Where you are now is not where you'll always be. Keep going.

—AKOSUA BOADI-AGYEMANG | BOTSWANA

"So, here you are
too foreign for home
too foreign for here.
never enough for both."

—IJEOMA UMEBINYUO, "DIASPORA BLUES"

CHAPTER 12

THE BRIDGE BETWEEN WORLDS

———

CROSSROADS

Nothing screams *"oh shit"* like the anxiety-ridden faces of college students who are only a matter of months, weeks, or days away from graduating. It's the collective laments and the *panic* and *desperation* that are about to ensue once we receive our diplomas and hop on a one-way ticket into the *cluster-fucked shit-show* that is *the real world. How am I going to gauge progress without the structure of an institution to guide me and keep me accountable? How am I going to pay off my student loans or pay back my parents for all the money they've invested in my education? How do I file my taxes? How am I going to move out all of my stuff? What do I do with this seventh edition of* History in Ancient Rome *I just wasted $100 on?*

Between the international students, it's also the solemness of the separation we all know is about to come once we all walk across that stage and step inside that airport one last time. For some, it's the sadness of having to say goodbye to a place we've called home for the past few years, and all the people who have helped define it as such. For others, it's the pain of being torn by the desire to chase after money and a career on one side of the world, but also wanting to be with friends and family on the other. It's the insecurity of whether or not some relationships can withstand the test of time and distance apart, the fear of becoming too far detached from our cultural roots, and the uncertainty of what lies ahead once our student visas are up.

IS THE GRASS REALLY GREENER ON THE OTHER SIDE?

Amongst the international students, there's always been this unspoken understanding at the back of everyone's minds that failing to secure employment sponsorship in the anglosphere and having to move back to our home countries after graduation would be considered a waste of our education and all the money our parents have spent to send us there. The default assumption has always been—*unless you're **that** fucking rich that you can just go home and take over a flourishing family business your parents have already set up for you to inherit since before you could even walk, or you just prefer the easier life back home which would somewhat indicate to others you lack ambition*—you *are* going to get a full-time job in your host country once you graduate and at least work there for a couple of years before moving back.

If you're lucky enough, you wouldn't even have to move back; you could be selected for permanent residency or citizenship (*or marry yourself into it*) and be given the chance to fight for a better life in a "better country." That's always been the glorified track we're set up to follow; some of us have never really been given the space to consider what the alternatives even are, and if those too could be as rewarding, if not perhaps more. I had a business professor during the second semester of my third year who, in the middle of lecturing us, said we should push ourselves harder and take advantage of all the entrepreneurial opportunities available to us in the United States. I will never forget the way he looked at me and said in front of the entire class, *"It would be such a shame for you to waste all of your potential after being here, just to go back to a country like Indonesia."*

Actually, Indonesia is the largest economy in all of Southeast Asia; it's the second-fastest growing G20 economy behind China, one of the biggest emerging economies on the planet, and we've been that way for many years now.[56] It's not that opportunity and economic potential in Indonesia and many other countries around the world are insufficient, it's just that they've gone largely unnoticed by Western and international media. Yes, there is plenty of opportunity to be great and succeed in the US, UK, Canada, and Australia, but the same is true in other countries outside of the anglosphere and the West as well. *There is opportunity everywhere around the world; you either find it if it already exists or make it if it doesn't. That's the whole point of being entrepreneurial.* Even from an employment standpoint, there are plenty of opportunities in other countries to climb up corporate ladders and break glass ceilings. Other countries present plenty of opportunities to lead, inspire, grow, explore the world, try new things, and be closer to family and other loved ones. All these things that can be just as valuable to one individual as a higher paycheck is to another.

---

56 "The World Bank In Indonesia: Overview" The World Bank, Last Updated October 1, 2020.

You'll always be grappling with the thought of how the grass is always greener on the other side. You can't help but ruminate on the thought of *what could have been* had you chosen to go the other direction. I think as international students, even we sometimes get stuck in this narrow mind-set that the whole world just revolves around the West, and there isn't anything really out there for us if we leave. It's taken me coming back to the side where, admittedly, I always thought the grass was going to be less green to finally realize it actually isn't. *The grass on the other side isn't greener, it's just different.* Perhaps it's a different shade of green, but at the end of the day, it's still green, and it'll always be green wherever you water it.

Yeah, I wanted that investment banking job with the nice LA apartment and five- to six-figure salary all to myself, and I did come back to Jakarta for the first few months bitter at my unemployment, feeling like I was robbed of my life (albeit mostly due to the pandemic). I do still find myself wondering about what that life would have been like from time to time, but now for the most part, I actually don't mind that I ended up not getting what I wanted because it's brought me here. I got to write this book and share the stories of my life, as well as the lives of my friends and other people just like me, which have hopefully touched the hearts of hundreds, thousands, or maybe even millions of people at home currently reading this.

BEST FOR THE WORLD

My international education has always taught me to be the *best for the world.* In fact, that was the motto of the school I graduated from in Jakarta. I remember reading over those words on the day of my high school commencement, not really sure what it was supposed to actually mean other than being some fluffy, feel-good marketing phrase. It was years later siting in that lecture room and listening to what that professor just said, to finally understand what that motto really meant.

∗ ∗ ∗

As international students, we've had the privilege of seeing so much of the world that we've not only seen what *it* has to offer *us*, but also what *we* have to offer *it*. Because we're always told we're the bridge that connects cultures, ideas, countries, and people from different worlds, I think sometimes we misunderstand it to mean we need to consistently be hopping from one place to another in order to gauge that bridging process. Becoming the *best for the world* doesn't mean being the best for *the whole world*, it's being the best for the world *we live in*. It doesn't mean becoming someone who is able to be everywhere at once, it's becoming someone who is able to bring a little bit of everywhere to just one place. The question for you is where is that one place going to be?

Is it going to be somewhere new and thrilling, far more progressive, developed, and glamorous, and you go there not only for the promise of a better life for yourself and your loved ones, but also to challenge yourself and push against boundaries?

Or is it going to be somewhere old and familiar, somewhere you grew up knowing all your life, is less thrilling, less progressive, less developed, and less glamorous, but you return with the hopes that, one day, you could be the one to turn it all around?

I'm in no way trying to paint those who choose to remain in the anglosphere and start a new life there as selfish people only interested in looking out for themselves, nor am I trying paint those who choose to return to their home countries as altruistic humanitarians either. At the end of the day, we're all just striving to make a contribution, to find our places in this world, leave our marks, and become a part of something much bigger than just ourselves, regardless of *where* we strive to do that from. Deep down, we all have a little bit of "I want to save the world" inside us, but the truth is not *all of us* have the luxury of time and money to go beyond just saving ourselves, and that's okay. What I'm saying is for those of us who *do* have that kind of privilege and have it in us to "save the world," it is perhaps worth considering which world we would like to save—because we can't save all of it.

I always knew from the moment I first set foot on US soil that, sooner or later, I—*by my own free will*—wanted to return to Indonesia because if all of us just go off to live in countries like the US, UK, Canada, or Australia and join all of the bright minds already there, then who's going to be left to fix our problems back home? *We can't all just leave.* What's going to be left of a country without any of its smart, skilled, and educated citizens to come back and give it hope for the future? The beauty of our education lies in not only how it has allowed us to envision what that future could look like, but to actually go out and see it with our own eyes as well. So, if we *are* able to bring back the progress and innovation we've seen out there, and give the country and community that have raised us the same chance of experiencing the better side of life the way we've had, then why don't we? Sure, I can't save the whole world. I won't be the one to save the world there, but I could be the one to save the world here, and that counts for something.

As much as I've talked about how other countries need internationals who have had the privilege of a Western education to come back *here*, the anglosphere also needs internationals who have had the privilege of cultural awareness, multilingualism, and a global perspective to stay *there*. The world needs every single one of us to bring back a little bit of everything from everywhere and to add to its richness by sharing our perspectives, experiences, discoveries, challenging the limits of envisioning what is possible, and that's how we all play our parts in creating a more interconnected and unified world. With that last line, comes the overarching message of this final chapter: *no matter where on earth our post-student lives take us to next, whether it's to ultimately go back home, or go live somewhere new, we may be far in distance from friends, family, and loved ones, but we'll always be together in the collective pursuit of bridging and building a better world from wherever we are in it.*

CLOSING REMARKS

Know that it's been nothing short of a testament to your strength, courage, and patience that you have crossed vast oceans and travelled far distances all on your own. You have had to go live in a new country, learn to speak a new language, adapt to a new culture, endure the pain of being apart from loved ones, and leapt over hurdles of legislation and prejudice, with the kind of grace and poise far beyond what most people your age are able to do. You have stood brave in the face of adversity, demonstrated a great deal of tenacity, adaptability, resilience, and proven yourself worthy of standing where you are now. Despite what anybody tells you or how they make you feel, stand firm in the knowledge you are *indeed* one of globalization's best byproducts, and the embodiment of what it means to be a global citizen, untethered by the limitations of national borders and cultural barriers.

Our time as international students is transient. I've been one my entire life, and now that I'm not, I look back and it's as if it was over in a blink of an eye. If I could relive everything from the beginning, not to change anything but to experience it all over again for the first time, I would. The heartbreaks that came with goodbyes and the disappointments in all the *what-ifs* and *could-have-beens* were the prices I have been—and would always be—willing to pay in exchange for everything else this kind of education has given me. Indeed, it is the gift of being an international student that despite coming from all different walks of life where we would have otherwise never met, there we were, against all the odds, meeting each other for the first time, and walking down the same path together. What a privilege it has been that I have had the opportunity to travel far and wide and meet someone like you, that we'll always get to take a piece of each other with us wherever farewells take us to next, and now we are on different shores finding our own shades of green.

Whether it's a mere few minutes away, or a *whole ass transcontinental flight* to the other side of where you are now, there *really is* a bigger world out there for you. It's always felt like there isn't anywhere out there that would accept you fully as you are, but wherever the soles of your feet touch the earth is exactly where you belong, and no one can take that away from you. Wherever life takes you after this, I hope you feel at home. I hope it treats you with kindness. I hope it receives you with open arms, and it's everything you've ever dreamed of. I hope you remember no matter where or how far you go, there will always be another life waiting to welcome you back on the other side. More than anything else, I hope you find a purpose that fulfills you and does right by the values you believe in and the people you love, so when you look back and ask yourself if everything you've gained to be right there where you are was worth everything you've had to give up and leave behind, the answer is always yes.

If you've made it this far, thank you. This book has truly been the culmination of years of hard work, heartache, *and a whole lot of hard liquor*. I hope somewhere in my little journey, you got to see yourself reflected in it as well. Being an international student has been the most rewarding experience of my life, and it will always be my greatest honor that I have had the opportunity to serve this lifetime with you as the bridge between worlds.

Don't worry. It gets better,
then bad, then worse, then much worse,
way, way worse, God awful,
what-in-the-fresh-hell awful,
and then, surprisingly, just okay, and then good,
and then it gets better again.

SPECIAL
ACKNOWLEDGMENTS

———

TO MY MOTHER

You are the classic tale of a "strong independent woman who don't need no man," and everything I've ever known about being an outspoken, fearless, and unapologetic bad bitch, I've had the honor of learning from you. Thank you for giving me the most beautiful, adventurous, and colorful life any kid could've possibly dreamed of...

...and the $6,000 you willingly donated to fund this book.

TO CLAIRE C. & TRISHA V., THE "LADY CLOWNS"

If it weren't for the limited amount of space I have for this acknowledgment, I would, as specifically requested by you clowns, write this in loving memory of my dead friends... except you two are still very much alive...and for that, I am grateful for every day. You two are my rocks, my compass, and my safe space from the world. My proudest accomplishment from JIS will always be that I graduated as your friend.

TO DAVID K., DIANDRA T., & MATTHEW O., "MY KIDS"

From Jakarta to Los Angeles and back, you three have consistently been my little pieces of home. It's been one of my greatest joys watching you guys grow up next to me, and that I'll always get to do so for the rest of my life (whether you like it or not). You make me proud every day, and I hope you always remember that.

TO ABRAHAM S., GLORIA S., MICHELLE N., & SABRINA C.

America has become a second home, largely in part because of you. Thank you for all the ways you've always made me feel like I was welcomed, and that I belonged.

TO JENNA N., JENNIFER C., KAREN T., MADHURI T., & SYLVIA Y.

You guys are the best thing to have ever come out of international orientation at LMU (besides that one trip to Disneyland). I'm looking forward to having you guys be my private tour guides when I come to visit Vietnam, India, Botswana, and China.

TO DIVYA A.

One could only be so lucky to receive the level of kindness, encouragement, and attentiveness you have given me over the years without ever being asked to give anything back in return. You will always have me to come home to.

TO MIKA. S., "COOKIE"

Thank you for all those years, even after high school, you continued to write me letters, which I still keep in my bedside drawers. Here's to future sleepovers and travel adventures around the world together.

TO NATASHA A.

To think our friendship started with an anxious email from fresh-off-the-plane college freshman Indah, asking you to help her figure out how to use the imperial system of measurements for a class assignment. It's so laughably on brand. Ever since then, it has been years of unwavering support, compassion, and companionship that I will always feel undeserving of. You are my number one hype-girl, and I appreciate you in ways that are profound.

TO MY FORMER VIETNAMESE AMERICAN ROOMMATE, "K"

I think if you and I had met a little later in life, we could have made more memories with each other than just petty and immature little impressions. Despite our miscommunications and misunderstandings, you've continued to remain a supportive friend to me all these years, which will always be the thing I respect and appreciate about you the most.

Thank you to all my beta-readers: **Abraham S., Anastasia R., Ashane G., Claire C., David K., Diandra T., Divya A., Ellaine P., Jessica T., Karen T., Kevin T., Luke B., Maika K., Madhuri T., Matthew O., Natasha A., Nathan T., Rebecca S., Sabrina C., Trisha V.** *Thank you for all of the feedback, comments, suggestions, and insights you've contributed to my draft revisions.*

Thank you to **Ronny Chieng and Tammy Duckworth,** *for giving me a chance.*

Thank you to my editor **Paige B.** *for the guidance, compassion, and comfort you've provided me during this very arduous—but rewarding—process.*

APPENDIX

INTRODUCTION

Mayberry, Kate. "Third Culture Kids: Citizens of everywhere and nowhere." *BBC*. November 19, 2016. https://www.bbc.com/worklife/article/20161117-third-culture-kids-citizens-of-everywhere-and-nowhere.

CHAPTER 1

Banerjee, Rupa, Jeffrey G. Reitz, and Phil Oreopoulos. "Do Large Employers Treat Racial Minorities More Fairly? An Analysis of Canadian Field Experiment Data." *Canadian Public Policy / Analyse De Politiques* Vol. 44, No. 1 (2018): 2–4. https://www.jstor.org/stable/90019784.

Marianne, Bertrand, and Sendhil Mullainathan. "Are Emily and Greg More Employable than Lakisha and Jamal? A Field Experiment on Labor Market Discrimination." *The American Economic Review* Vol. 94, No. 4 (2004): 991–1013. https://www.jstor.org/stable/3592802.

CHAPTER 2

"Communicating Across Borders: How Well Do Indonesians Speak English?" *Indonesia Investments*. August 7, 2017. https://www.indonesia-investments.com/news/todays-headlines/communicating-across-borders-how-well-do-indonesians-speak-english/item8072.

Du Monteil, Eva. "Which Language Has The Most Words?." *Babbel Magazine,* February 1, 2020. https://www.babbel.com/en/magazine/language-most-words.

Kaur, Harmeet. "A Duke professor warned Chinese students to speak English." *CNN.* January 29, 2019.

https://edition.cnn.com/2019/01/28/health/duke-professor-warns-chinese-students-speak-english-trnd/index.html.

Laycock, Stuart. "All the Countries We've Ever Invaded: And the Few We Never Got Round To." *History Press.* 2012.

Statista. "The Most Spoken Languages Worldwide in 2019." Publication November 27, 2020. https://www.statista.com/statistics/266808/the-most-spoken-languages-worldwide/.

CHAPTER 3

Quora. "Why Do Indonesian People Look Like Half-Asian and Half-African?." Publication July 17, 2020. https://www.quora.com/Why-do-Indonesian-people-look-like-half-Asian-and-half-African.

Yuniarni, Sarah. "Unity in Diversity: Indonesia's Six Largest Ethnic Groups." *Jakarta Globe,* July 16, 2016. https://jakartaglobe.id/lifestyle/unity-diversity-indonesias-six-largest-ethnic-groups/.

CHAPTER 4

Bennett, James. "The Emerging Anglosphere. (America and the West)." *ORBIS* Vol. 46, No. 1 (2001): 111–126. https://link.gale.com/apps/doc/A82270185/AONE?u=loym48904&sid=AONE&xid=d8f133c2.

Coban, Filiz. "The Role of the Media in International Relations: From the CNN Effect to the Al-Jazeere Effect." *Journal of International Relations and Foreign Policy* Vol. 4, No. 2 (2016): 45–61 http://jirfp.com/journals/jirfp/Vol_4_No_2_December_2016/3.pdf.

Geonet at the Oxford Internet Institute. "Digital Hegemonies: The Localness of Search Engine Results." Published May 4, 2017. http://geonet.oii.ox-.ac.uk/blog/digital-hegemonies-the-localness-of-search-engine-results/.

Graham, Mark and Anasuya Sengupta."We're all connected now, so why is the internet so white and Western?" *The Guardian.* Published October

5, 2017. https://www.theguardian.com/commentisfree/2017/oct/05/internet-white-western-google-wikipedia-skewed.

ICEF Monitor. "Annual survey finds continued growth in international schools." Publication September 5, 2018. https://monitor.icef.com/2018/09/annual-survey-finds-continued-growth-in-international-schools/.

ISC Research. "About The International Schools Market." Accessed February 6, 2021. https://www.iscresearch.com/about-us/the-market.

Kraidy, M. "Globalization of culture through the media. In J. R. Schement (Ed.)" *Encyclopedia of Communication and Information* Vol. 2 (2002): 359–363. http://repository.upenn.edu/asc_papers/325.

Roberts, Andrews. "It's Time to Revive the Anglosphere." *The Wall Street Journal.* August 8, 2020. https://www.wsj.com/articles/its-time-to-revive-the-anglosphere-11596859260.

Select USA. "The Media and Entertainment Industry in the United States." Accessed February 6, 2021. https://www.selectusa.gov/media-entertainment-industry-united-states.

Statista. "The 15 Countries with the Highest Military Spending Worldwide in 2019." Publication December 1, 2020. https://www.statista.com/statistics/262742/countries-with-the-highest-military-spending/.

The World Bank. "United States." Accessed February 6, 2021. https://data.worldbank.org/country/US.

Windaningrum, Ethenia. "OK, So You Are A Proud Indonesian, but Are You A Confident Indonesian?" *Kompasiana* (Blog). June 24, 2015. https://www.kompasiana.com/niathenia/5528e81b6ea834ac288b45e5/ok-so-you-are-a-proud-indonesian-but-are-you-a-confident-indonesian.

World Population Review. "Jakarta Population 2021." Accessed February 6, 2021. https://worldpopulationreview.com/world-cities/jakarta-population.

CHAPTER 5

Ahn, Yong Yeol, Sebastian E. Ahnert, James P. Bagrow and Albert-László Barabási. "Flavor Network and The Principles of Food Pairing." *Scientific Report.* Vol.1, No.196 (2011). https://doi.org/10.1038/srep00196.

Eating Utensils. "Facts and History of Eating Utensils." Accessed on February 26, 2016. http://www.eatingutensils.net.

Statista. "Leading countries based on the production of milled rice in 2018/2019 (in million metric tons)." Publication February 2020. https://www.statista.com/statistics/255945/top-countries-of-destination-for-us-rice-exports-2011/.

CHAPTER 6

Couvillion, Marion B. and Sue S. Minchew. "A Comparison of American and International Students' Lifestyles and Perceptions of the University Experience." *National Forum of Applied Educational Research Journal.* No. 16, No. 3 (2003). https://citeseerx.ist.psu.edu/viewdoc/download?-doi=10.1.1.621.3171&rep=rep1&type=pdf.

Doubek, James. "Attention, Students: Put Your Laptops Away." *NPR.* Publication April 17, 2016. https://www.npr.org/2016/04/17/474525392/attention-students-put-your-laptops-away.

Vandrick, Stephanie. "Language, Culture, Class, Gender, and Class Participation." (2000): 2–11. https://www.researchgate.net/publication/234628161_Language_Culture_Class_Gender_and_Class_Participation.

CHAPTER 7

Carter, Dorinda J. "Why the Black Kids Sit Together at the Stairs: The Role of Identity-Affirming Counter-Spaces in a Predominantly White High School." *The Journal of Negro Education* Vol. 76, No. 4 (2007): 542–4. https://www.jstor.org/stable/40037227.

Ehrlich, Paul R., David S. Dobkin, and Darryl Wheye. "Mixed-Species Flocking." Stanford University. March 12, 2021. https://web.stanford.edu/group/stanfordbirds/text/essays/Mixed-Species_Flocking.html.

McPherson, Miller, Lynn Smith-Lovin, and James M. Cook. "Birds of A Feather: Homophily in Social Networks." *Annual Review of Sociology,* Vol. 27 (2001): 415–444 https://www.jstor.org/stable/2678628

CHAPTER 8

Ritter, Zachary S. "Taboo or Tabula Rasa: Cross-Racial/Cultural Dating Preferences amongst Chinese, Japanese, and Korean International Students in an American University." *Journal of International Students.* Vol. 5, No. 4 (2015): 405–419. https://files.eric.ed.gov/fulltext/EJ1066278.pdf.

CHAPTER 9

Bejanyan, Kathrine, Tara C. Marshall, and Nelli Ferenczi. "Romantic ideals, mate preferences, and anticipation of future difficulties in marital life: a comparative study of young adults in India and America." *Frontiers in Psychology*. Vol. 5 (2014): 2. https://www.frontiersin.org/article/10.3389/fpsyg.2014.01355.

Cherry, Kendra. "Understanding Collectivist Cultures." March 24, 2020. https://www.verywellmind.com/what-are-collectivistic-cultures-2794962.

Nesteruk, Olena and Alexandra Gramescu. "Dating and Mate Selection Among Young Adults from Immigrant Families." *Marriage & Family Review*. Vol. 48, No. 1: 40–58. https://doi-org.electra.lmu.edu/10.1080/0 1494929.2011.620732.

Ritter, Zachary S. "Taboo or Tabula Rasa: Cross-Racial/Cultural Dating Preferences amongst Chinese, Japanese, and Korean International Students in an American University." *Journal of International Students* Vol. 5, No. 4 (2015): 405-419. https://files.eric.ed.gov/fulltext/EJ1066278.pdf .

CHAPTER 10

Albrecht, Leslie. "Harry Potter at 20: How J.K. Rowling went from welfare to billion-dollar wizards." *MarketWatch*. June 27,2017. https://www.marketwatch.com/story/harry-potter-at-20-how-jk-rowling-went-from-welfare-to-wizards-2017-06-26.

D'Angelo, Chris. "How Obama's 'Brutal' First Job Inspired A New Youth Employment Initiative." *HuffPost*. Updated December 19, 2016. https://www.huffpost.com/entry/obama-first-job-baskin-robbins_n_56d100afe4b-0871f60eb8c5a.

Potter, Emmy. "How Hugh Jackman Went From Teaching PE To Wolverine." *Looper*, April 21, 2017. https://www.looper.com/59508/hugh-jackman-went-teaching-pe-wolverine/?utm_campaign=clip

Sanchez, Omar. "Drake is Spotify's most-streamed artist of the decade." *EntertainmentWeekly*, December 3, 2019. https://ew.com/music/2019/12/03/drake-most-streamed-artist-2010s-spotify/.

CHAPTER 11

Australian Government, Trade and Investment Commission. "Education Data: Monthly Summary of International Student data (YTD November 2020)." Accessed February 26, 2021. https://www.austrade.gov.au/Australian/Education/Education-data/Current-data/summaries-and-news.

El-Assal, Kareem. "642,000 international students: Canada now ranks 3rd globally in foreign student attraction." *CIC News*. Published on February 20th, 2020. https://www.cicnews.com/2020/02/642000-international-students-canada-now-ranks-3rd-globally-in-foreign-student-attraction-0213763.html#gs.u1ae99.

Government of Canada. "Post-Graduation Work Permit Program (PGWPP)." Accessed February 26, 2021. https://www.canada.ca/en/immigration-refugees-citizenship/corporate/publications-manuals/operational-bulletins-manuals/temporary-residents/study-permits/post-graduation-work-permit-program.html.

"International Student Statistics in UK 2020." *Study in UK* Accessed February 26, 2021. https://www.studying-in-uk.org/international-student-statistics-in-uk/#:~:text=A%20total%20of%20342%2C620%20students,European%20Union%2C%20excluding%20the%20UK.

Marginson, Simon. "The UK in the global student market: second place for how much longer?." *Centre For Global Higher Education*. Published July 19, 2018. https://www.researchcghe.org/perch/resources/publications/the-uk-in-the-global-student-market.pdf.

Open Doors. "Enrollment Trends: International Student Data From The 2020 Open Doors Report." Accessed February 26, 2021. https://opendoorsdata.org/data/international-students/enrollment-trends/.

Redden, Elizabeth. "International Student Numbers Decline." *Inside Higher Ed*. Publication January 22, 2018. https://www.insidehighered.com/news/2018/01/22/nsf-report-documents-declines-international-enrollments-after-years-growth.

SGM Law Group. "H-1B Lottery 2019-2020 | Results, Process, and Chances (Updated 4/12/19)." Publication April 12, 2019. https://www.immi-usa.com/h1b-lottery-2016-results-chances-process/.

Shelton, Jacob. "Crazy Odds That Will Surprise You." *Ranker.* Accessed February 26, 2021. https://www.ranker.com/list/weird-odds-and-statistics/jacob-shelton.

"Temporary Graduate visa (subclass 485) Post-Study Work Stream." *Australian Government Department of Home Affairs.* Accessed February 26, 2021. https://immi.homeaffairs.gov.au/visas/getting-a-visa/visa-listing/temporary-graduate-485/post-study-work.

CHAPTER 12
The World Bank. "The World Bank In Indonesia: Overview." Last Updated October 1, 2020. https://www.worldbank.org/en/country/indonesia/overview.

Printed in Great Britain
by Amazon

65456747R00149